CRASH COURSE

on
Money Smarts

15
LAWS OF MANAGING MONEY AND CREATING WEALTH

COUNTRYMAN

A Division of Thomas Nelson Publishers
Since 1798

www.thomasnelson.com

CRASH COURSE

on
Money Smarts

15
LAWS OF
MANAGING
MONEY
AND CREATING
WEALTH

Table of Contents

Foreword

To the Reader:

One person can make an average income, nothing extraordinary, and turn it into millions. Another can make three times as much and end up broke. This is a curious phenomenon, isn't it? It would seem wealthy people get that way because they either made a huge salary, inherited bundles, or they received a windfall from an invention, lucky investment, or the lottery.

But, no. When you look into how people got rich, very few did so because they had some amazing talent or fortunate money bonanza. Rather, they accumulated money by acquiring knowledge about money and establishing smart money habits.

What you are really going to like about this book is that you can use the information in it to do the same. If your desire is to be a millionaire, you can use it for that. If you need to clean up your credit and become debt free, you will find out exactly what you need to do. You will even find the information in this book on how to finance a house, save for your children's college education and retire comfortably.

This book is especially useful for those of us who are confused about insurance, investing, and credit. The author, Lisa Tresch, does a wonderful job of taking these important, complex subjects and explaining them without putting you into a deep sleep. Instead, when you read this book, you'll probably find yourself saying, "Really? I didn't know that. Now that I do know it, I can take the information and put it to use right away!"

Financial freedom and even great wealth are well within the grasp of just average individuals. This is really good news. The only question that remains is, "Will you become one of the financially free ones or one of the financially strapped ones?" The answer to the question will be determined by how well you come to know and employ the fifteen laws of managing money and creating wealth in this book.

On that journey down the road to financial autonomy, I wish you Godspeed!

Sincerely,

Larry J. Koenig, Ph.D.

General Editor and Series Consultant

You and Your Money

*In all realms of life it takes courage
to stretch your limits, express your power,
and fulfill your potential.
It's no different in the financial realm.*

—SUZE ORMAN

POWER STATEMENT:

Playing it smart with your money doesn't have to be complicated and time-consuming when you understand some basic money laws and put them into place.

Everyone has a money IQ. For some people, ignorance is bliss. They would rather not know how much money they really have, where it's going, or where it's been. As long as the credit card will swipe and the creditors aren't calling, they prefer to keep the financial picture blurred and enjoy life. At the other extreme are those who watch every penny and scrutinize each expenditure. They closely follow the stock market and invest in real estate and worry about bull and bear markets with an obsession that keeps them awake at night.

Somewhere between these two extremes is the person who has decided to play it smart with his money and enjoy life at the same time. It is possible. Unfortunately, many people don't know enough about spending, saving, budgeting, investing, planning for the future, and other elements of financial planning that create a solid financial foundation, and so they can only enjoy life until the money runs out. And, let's be honest, there are probably some of us that don't want to know about these things. We would rather schedule a root canal than create a budget or think about retirement investments.

If you aren't sure where you fall on the money IQ spectrum, take a few moments to answer these simple questions:

- Do you budget your money?
- Do you pay off your credit cards each month?
- Do you have a savings account? Retirement fund? Investment accounts?
- Do you protect your money with insurance?
- Do you plan for big-ticket purchases or do you buy on impulse?
- Do you have a long-term plan for your money?

This crash course will give you the ability to understand your money, make it work for you, and avoid the pitfalls that could wreck your financial stability. It will show you that developing money smarts doesn't have to be complicated. Budgeting, investing, and planning for retirement doesn't involve intricate accounting calculations, and you don't need a head-spinning education on the stock market in order to invest your money. But you do need to follow a few laws and stick to them if you want to brighten your financial future.

Here are two examples that illustrate the importance of having money smarts:

Beth is five years out of college and worse off financially than before she graduated. She grew up watching her parents spend more money than they earned. Her father was always working on the next get-rich-quick scheme, and her mother spent money they didn't have in antique shops and flea markets. Beth grew up without a concept of savings, and because her parents had not planned for college tuition, she was saddled with hefty student loans after graduation. She was constantly taking cash advances on her credit card to pay rent, so she couldn't imagine how she could afford to start saving anything.

Beth believed that someday in the distant, fuzzy future, when she got her finances in order, she would start setting back money to buy a house. The thought of saving for retirement seemed absurd.

FAST FACTS:

Every day, $3 trillion passes through the trading desks and clearing operations of JPMorganChase, and that's just one of thousands of banks in the U.S.

How could she possibly think that far ahead when she was scrounging every spare penny just to make ends meet?

Since she didn't have a concept of budgeting, she never seemed to know where her money had been, how much she had, or how much she would need for the next month. Five years after college, Beth's credit card debt had escalated and her minimum-payment mentality had her on track for a lifetime of credit card payments. She was staring at what seemed like an eternity buried under the burden of her student loans and living in the same apartment because she knew she couldn't qualify for a mortgage loan with her terrible credit history. Beth spent most weeks crossing her fingers that her credit line would keep her safe, and praying that she didn't have any unexpected expenditures.

Rob is five years out of college and in contrast to Beth, is in a comfortable financial position and able to enjoy life without fretting over his finances. He grew up in a family that also never seemed to have enough money, but his father made certain that the same thing wouldn't happen to his son. He taught him the importance of saving money, cautious spending, and planning for the future.

DID YOU KNOW?

In 2005, personal bankruptcies soared to an all-time high as people rushed to file before new restrictions were put into place. Nearly 2.1 million debtors set the record, up 30 percent from the previous year. It was the largest number of bankruptcy petitions ever filed in a 12-month period in the history of the federal courts.

Rob's parents also couldn't pay for his college tuition, and like Beth, he graduated with a sizable loan burden. Each month, however, Rob set aside a small amount of money to pay down the college loan debt and save for a house. He was careful not to let his credit card balance accumulate, and he opted into his company's 401K matching contribution retirement account, even though he could have used the extra paycheck amount each month for something else. Because his credit was good, in a few years Rob was able to qualify for a home mortgage loan to purchase a two-bedroom house near his office. He received a small raise, and decided to take the extra money and invest in an index fund. After a few years, his savings began to earn compounded interest, and Rob could see that the small amount of money that he had invested was growing quite nicely.

The stories of Beth and Rob are examples of how a small amount of money smarts can make a big difference for the present and the future. Many Americans, like Beth, have never been exposed to money-smart laws. Her paycheck-to-paycheck existence is discouraging, but by learning and implementing the money-smart laws, everyone in Beth's position has the ability to improve their money IQ and their financial health.

PERSONAL REFLECTION:

What did you learn about money growing up, and how has that shaped your attitude toward finances? Do you worry about money? If so, how is it affecting your life in other areas, like your relationships and your work life?

✓ YOUR TO DO LIST:

Rate your money IQ based on the list of questions in the introduction. If you answered no to two or more of the questions, write down three goals you'd like to accomplish to improve your financial picture.

PART I

THE BASICS

Know Your Worth

Do what you can,
with what you have,
where you are.
—THEODORE ROOSEVELT

POWER STATEMENT:

In order to begin developing money smarts, you will need to know your net worth and understand your cash flow so that you have a clear picture of your financial health.

Many people have no idea what they are worth—financially, that is. A ballpark figure of what you have in your checking account is not your net worth. Neither is the amount you can charge on your credit card. So what is the big deal about net worth and why should anyone take the time to sit down and calculate it?

Simply put, your net worth is a clear and realistic picture of your financial situation. It tells you how much true wealth you have, and it can be a gauge that helps you manage your money.

According to a study released by the Consumer Federation of America and the Financial Planning Association, only about half of adults know what personal net worth is. Even after they were given the definition of personal net worth, 48 percent of respondents indicated they couldn't even give an approximation of their net worth, and 21 percent of them believed that the most practical way to accumulate several hundred thousand dollars was to win the lottery.[1]

If you are hoping for an unexpected, out-of-the-blue cash windfall to solve all your money worries, reality is grim: You have a better chance of getting in a plane crash or struck by lightning than winning the lottery. In fact, the odds are around 80 million to one per lottery ticket. People play the lottery anyway in the hopes of striking it rich, yet they don't realize that developing a plan for growing the money you already do have and then sticking to that plan is the best road to financial security.

Calculating your net worth is the starting point in developing money smarts. Here's the basic definition: Net worth is the difference between what you own (assets) and what you owe (liabilities). Assets are cash and other property with monetary value. Liabilities are the debts that you owe.

Assets

There are three different kinds of assets you need to know about to calculate your net worth. Liquid assets are anything that can be liquidated, or turned into cash, immediately. Some examples include your checking account balance, your savings and money market account balances, cash value life insurance, and any other asset that has the same value as cash.

In order to get a handle on your liquidity, you should gather the statements and total your liquid assets. Personal assets and other possessions include the current market value of your home, the market value of your cars, your furniture, jewelry, electronic equipment, and any other personal items that have immediate monetary value. List your personal assets and possessions and then add up their value.

Investment assets are savings certificates or CDs, stocks, bonds, Individual Retirement Accounts (IRAs), mutual funds, and any other investments. When you total your assets, the number probably looks pretty good.

Now it's time to look at the flip side of your financial picture.

Liabilities

The two types of liabilities are current liabilities and long-term liabilities. Your current liabilities include credit card debt and any loan balances you might have, such as student loans or car loans. Long-term liabilities include your mortgage and any other debt that you pay over a long period of time. Add the long-term liabilities to your current liabilities, and then subtract the total from that good-looking number you came up with when you added up your assets.

Many people measure their financial health by looking solely at the asset side instead of calculating what they are worth, according to *Washington Post* financial columnist Michelle Singletary.[2] If your assets look pretty good—$50,000 of equity in your home, and maybe another $20,000 in other assets—but you have $80,000 in consumer debt (credit cards or car loans), your net worth is in negative territory, says Singletary. Each year, you should use your net worth calculation to determine how you are doing financially. If your net worth shrinks, you will know that you need to do things differently in the next twelve months. If your net worth grows, you will know that you are on the right track.

Cash Flow

In order to get a complete picture of your finances, you also need to understand your cash flow—or why your money seems to keep disappearing and where it is going. We'll talk more about this in Chapter Three, but the simple way to bring your cash flow into focus is to subtract your bills and expenditures from your income.

Linda wanted to find out why she never seemed to have money leftover at the end of each month. She was tired of resorting to her credit card to pay for things before the next paycheck arrived, so she determined that she would solve the mystery. For sixty days, she kept a piece of paper in her purse and wrote down every dollar or cent that left her hand, even if was in the form of credit card charges and automatic bank withdrawals. She glanced at the paper at the end of the first month, and then took a close look at it after sixty days. She took the figures and then categorized her spending so she could see what areas of her life were costing her the most money. Linda realized that she spent around $280 over her income both months, an amount that ended up on her steadily increasing credit card bill.

It's important, when analyzing cash flow, to keep in mind that there are some expenses that occur infrequently and should be factored in as well. Car insurance payments usually are due every six months. Renter's insurance, property tax bills, Christmas and birthday expenses, and expected car maintenance should be included in the expense listing. Total these "hidden" expenses and divide the amount by twelve. This should give you an average monthly expense amount that you can add in with your expected monthly expenses. Keep in mind that this total doesn't have to be exact to the penny,

FAST FACTS:

According to the Federal Reserve's Report on U.S. Family Finances, the net worth of the typical American family rose only 1.5% after inflation between 2001 and 2004, the Federal Reserve said in an update of a survey it does once every three years. The Fed said the net worth of the median American family—the one smack in the statistical middle—was $93,100 in 2004. Net worth, the difference between a family's assets and liabilities, rose a robust 10.3% between 1998 and 2001 and 17.4% in the three-year interval before that.[3]

but it does need to reflect your cash flow as closely as you can approximate. If you want to get an even clearer picture of where your money is going, keep track of your expenses for six months.

Linda's cash flow analysis, along with the net worth calculations that she had already done, showed that she was living above her means, especially since her net worth was shockingly low. This clear picture of her finances was the jolt she needed to get her thinking seriously about a plan for her money. It also caused her to pause and consider the purchases she was tempted to make in a given week. She realized that each impulse purchase she made, such as the wicker settee that she saw in the antique store window (it set her back $175) affected her cash flow and ultimately her net worth.

DID YOU KNOW?

Half of American families have net financial assets under $1,000 and have modest or no net worth.[4]

According to Stephen Brobeck, the Consumer Federation of America's executive director, people who know their personal wealth are more likely to spend, borrow, and save sensibly. They tend to be more aware that overspending on a car diminishes their wealth, he says. Finding out the truth about your financial health can be a shocking exercise, but it can also be the motivation for taking a look at lifestyle and spending habits. It's easy to keep charging on the credit card and turning a blind eye to the empty wallet if you are unaware of your true financial state of affairs. If you have your net worth number in your head, you are probably not going to be so comfortable indulging in those expenses that you really can't afford.

Corporations regularly prepare balance sheets to determine their current net worth. It's imperative to the success of the business because owners can't make

CASE STUDY:

Andrea thought she had found the man of her dreams in David. Not only was he attentive, fun, and full of surprises, he was also a successful businessman. He drove an expensive convertible sports car, lived in a fancy condo with lavish furnishings, took exotic vacations, and ate only in the finest restaurants. Andrea was swept away by David, and when he proposed, she accepted.

They married and he paid for a honeymoon in Italy, but after a year of marriage, the honeymoon between them seemed to be over. Andrea had judged David's wealth only by his assets. She had no idea of his debts. Her financial picture of him was incomplete, but everything came into clear focus when David was forced to declare bankruptcy. He was so deep in debt from his expensive lifestyle that his debts eventually caught up with him. If Andrea had calculated those debts in with the wonderful assets that lured her into marriage, she would have realized that David's net worth was deep in negative numbers.

money decisions if they don't know where the business stands financially. It's the same for an individual or family. Wise money decisions are never made in ignorance. Preparing your own personal balance sheet, complete with net worth and cash flow, will help you gain control over your money and change how you make spending decisions. It will also give you the starting point for the next important money law: getting a money plan.

PERSONAL REFLECTION:

Are you making money decisions without a clear knowledge of your net worth and cash flow? Are you willing to make adjustments to your financial lifestyle after you calculate your net worth and cash flow?

✓ YOUR TO DO LIST:

Calculate your net worth. An easy way to do it: Go to www.Americasaves.org and click on Saver Resources. You can also prepare your own net worth balance sheet by using the sample worksheet in Appendix A. For the next two months, track your cash flow. Be sure to include those hidden expenses that might not show up during the sixty-day period. Appendix A includes a sample worksheet for a cash flow analysis.

FOR FURTHER STUDY:

What's Your Net Worth? Click Your Way to Wealth
   —by Jennifer Openshaw

Personal Cash Flow and Net Worth Planning Demystified
   —by Paul D. Kadavy

Get a Money Plan

*If you want to change your financial ways,
just change. Don't stop to analyze,
or to ask why or how. Just change.*

—SUZE ORMAN

POWER STATEMENT:

Setting specific and realistic
financial goals will allow you to
turn your money dreams into
realities.

E veryone needs a dream. There are some people who dream of retiring at age forty-five so they can travel and enjoy the good life. For others, their dream is simply to afford to buy a digital camera in the next year. Whether your dreams are long-term or short-term, the chances are good that some of them will cost money. And the chances are even better that it's money that you don't have in hand at the moment. So you will need a money plan.

Dreams are destined to stay locked away and out of reach unless they are attached to goals and then set in motion with plans. Setting solid goals that are realistic and attainable is the most reliable method of achieving wealth. Once you have goals in front of you and a plan to reach them, your mind becomes focused on achieving your dreams.

Mack's dream was two-fold. He wanted to get out of debt and have enough money to live abroad. It sounded simple enough, but he knew that in order to make it happen, he was going to have to come up with some kind of plan for gathering up the money. He had no rich relatives, and he wasn't a gambler, so he knew that his dream was going to involve some careful thought and realistic planning. The key would be sticking to the plan to make his dream reality.

Mack realized that he had been living haphazardly

when it came to his money. He had no plan for cutting back on his spending, and no goals for how much money he wanted to save in order to get out of debt and move overseas. Most of the time, he didn't know how much money he spent, and so his credit card balance continued to swell with each passing month. He felt like his money was out of control.

Having goals and a plan for reaching them prevents the kind of random financial lifestyle that Mack was living. Without a plan, most of the money that could be used for fulfilling our dreams is spent on impulse purchases or unneeded items, or on emergencies for which there is no cushion fund in place. It leaves us running in the same circles and never getting anywhere.

Turning our dreams into realities starts with defining the dreams, or making a wish list. If you want to build a cute little vacation cabin in the woods or have enough money to be philanthropic or pay for your triplets' college education, then you start by writing down those dreams. Be specific when you make your wish list. You should list some short-term dreams—such as remodeling the bathroom in the fall—as well as the long-term dreams. Mack's dreams were both short-term and long-term. He wanted to get out of debt within two years, and move abroad within ten years.

Financial advisor Judy Lawrence tells her clients that the first short-term goal should be to create an emergency or cushion fund (more about this in Chapter 7). The fund should have at least three months' take-home pay set aside as a protection against unforeseen problems or disasters.[1] Mack knew that when unexpected expenditures arose, his cushion fund would keep him from having to run up his credit card bill, which would set him back in his goal of becoming debt free. Once you have taken care of setting up a cushion fund, you will be ready to move on to planning for the things that comprise your wish list.

Specifics will help you when it comes to putting the plan in place. If you want to retire early, choose an age that you would like to set as a retirement goal. If your dream is to buy a boat and learn to sail, be specific about how much the boat and lessons will cost. Your plan will be easier to chart the more details you can provide about the amount of money you will need.

Saving for college tuition will involve finding some estimates for tuition costs in the years you will be sending Junior off to the university. Be sure and include a start and end date for each item on your wish list, but also be willing to keep things flexible. If one of your short-term dreams is to purchase a new laptop computer for your home office, choose a date that you will start working toward the purchase and an approximate date you will buy the computer. Your plan may include setting aside $100 each month from the fund usually reserved for eating out and entertainment expenses. If this is your plan, then you will also want to come up with some alternative cheaper strategies for entertainment so that you can meet your saving goal.

Part of your plan will involve deciding what short-term and long-term savings plans to use—mutual funds, bank savings account, stocks, Roth IRA, money market. We'll explain the different funds you can choose from in proceeding chapters, but for now you should know that wise investments of your money will be one of the keys to making your dream happen.

If you have family members, they need to be in on the wish list making. If your husband has no desire to travel the world after you both retire at age forty-five, but instead wants to buy a houseboat and live out his retirement on Lake Erie, then you probably should discuss this portion of your wish list until you reach a compromise. Family members may not be as excited about your dream of starting a dog-breeding business, so you should consult their lists as well and come up with some dreams that everyone can agree on.

Most of the time, dreams involve some sacrifice. As you make your wish list, keep in mind that you will need to determine how much and what kind of saving you will need in order to reach your goals. Setting back this money will probably involve some lifestyle change. You may have to switch from café lattes to generic brand coffee in a nice stainless steel travel mug, but keep in mind you can chunk that $1,220 into savings every year.

Once a dream is defined, the goals set out, and the plan in place, you will have more motivation to see your dream to its reality. When Mack wrote down his two goals, seeing them in black and white made them seem more possible. Once he began to

FAST FACTS:

According to a recent study, people who have control over their finances, particularly those with the propensity to plan and budget, are on average 39 percent wealthier than their less organized peers.[2]

do some research on what it would take to reach his goals and fulfill his dreams, Mack realized that with some time, patience, and discipline, he could make these two things happen. Suddenly, he felt more motivation about his financial goals than he had ever imagined. Every morning, he woke up and looked at his wish list, which he had posted on the bulletin board on his kitchen, and renewed his commitment to stick to his plan.

In addition to writing out his wish list, Mack made a financial goals worksheet for his two items.

Short Term Goals

Goal	Target Date	Cost Estimate	Amount Saved	Plan to Achieve

Long Term Goals

Goal	Target Date	Cost Estimate	Amount Saved	Plan to Achieve

Now he could clearly see the financial road that he would be traveling in order to meet his goals. Having that clear picture in his mind lessened Mack's chances that he would veer off the road. When he was tempted to spend money on something spontaneous that was a want instead of a need he remembered the plan and was able to put himself back on track.

Having a money plan will keep your financial life from spinning out of control. Like Mack, you will know that you have control, instead of feeling like unseen forces are controlling your money. You won't be surprised by credit card statements, and you won't have to wonder where all that extra money keeps going (you'll have it safely tucked away in wise investments). Mack was able to rest easy where his financial life was concerned because he knew that time was on his side. He had ten years to make his money work for him, and although he knew he wasn't going to become a millionaire in that amount of time, he knew that with patience he would see his money grow.

PERSONAL REFLECTION:

Do you have a plan for your money, or do you live a financially random lifestyle? Think about your money trail. Have you allowed money to "slip out the back door"? As you think about a wish list, begin to imagine what you could do with all the wayward money that is slipping through your fingers.

✓ *YOUR TO DO LIST:*

Make a wish list. Take fifteen minutes and a piece of paper and list all the things you would like to have or do. If you have family members, have them complete a list also and then compare the lists. Decide what items on the list the family will work toward.

Rank your wish list from most wanted to least wanted.

As you read the rest of this book, decide what you will need to do to make these dreams reality. Goal theorists say that goals should be made publicly, so once you have made your wish list and written down the goals, tell someone.

FOR FURTHER STUDY:

H&R Block's *Just Plain Smart Personal Finance Advisor: A Lifelong Approach to Achieving Your Financial Goals*

The Motley Fool Personal Finance Workbook
—by David Gardner and Tom Gardner

Create a Budget You Can Live With

---

*A budget tells us what
we can't afford,
but it doesn't keep us from buying it.*
—WILLIAM FEATHER

POWER STATEMENT:

Creating a budget that you control will lead to better money decisions by cutting out unnecessary expenditures and allowing you to concentrate on your money goals.

Let's talk budgets. Corporations must have them to make sure they are not spending more money than they are taking in; the government needs a budget to hold our leaders accountable; even filmmakers have to budget for a film so that they don't get to the halfway point and realize they can't finish production. And you need a budget for all of the same reasons. If governments and big business can't operate without a budget, you probably can't get along well without one either. You may hobble along for a while without budgeting, but it is likely that your financial issues will catch up with you.

Even if you are in the ranks of the wealthy, you need to watch your money coming and going. The reason is simple: You will have more money if you get control of your money. If you still unconvinced about the value of budgeting, here are four good reasons to do it:

- A budget will reveal whether you are living within your means or above it. Credit cards confuse us. We think we have more money than we actually do because if we're short of cash, then a charge card will allow us to buy things we can't afford. Numbers don't lie, however, and a budget will tell the truth about whether you can really afford that tenth pair of strappy sandals or the putting green for your home office.

- A budget will help you meet your savings goals. Left to our own devices, setting aside money for savings can be a Herculean task. Good intentions of putting money in a savings account get forgotten or postponed until next month. A budget includes a monthly mechanism for doing this, and once you have the budget set up, you don't have to make the decision. It's already been made for you.

• A budget guarantees that you will have money for emergencies or unexpected expenses. Life is full of surprises. Just when you think that everything is rocking along with steady precision, something comes along to tip the boat—and it often has a hefty price tag attached to it. You can't ignore the fact that water heaters bust and kids need dental work and transmissions go out on cars with expired warranties. A budget assures that you have money for all of life's little surprises.

• A budget forces you to distinguish between wants and needs. We live in an era of marketing experts who know how to blur the lines between what we need and what we think we need. Do you really need a flat screen TV? Or a leather jacket for your dog? There is nothing wrong with having things we want and indulging in luxury items if we can afford them. Marketers convince us we deserve to have these things even if we can't pay for them—which makes them seem like needs. A budget forces you to prioritize your spending and place your needs and wants in their proper category.

When you think of budgeting, do you have visions of evenings spent hunched over an adding machine as you pore over complicated spreadsheets and piles of receipts? For people who love the tedious business of numbers and accounting, this may be just the kind of budgeting they love to do, but for most of us, this is not our idea of fun, exciting long-term money management. Some people don't even like the word budget, so let's think of it in a different way. If you want to define what a budget actually is, think of it as a "spending and savings plan." You will be outlining (and sticking to!) a plan for spending your money and saving your money.

In Chapter 1 we discussed cash flow. Tracking your money for several months gives you some idea where your money is going. A budget tells you where your money should be going. The first step in creating a spending and savings plan that works for you is to determine how much money you make each month. This sounds obvious, but it's not quite as straightforward as it seems, especially if you get paid more than once a month. Use the chart below to calculate your salary:

Payment schedule	Multiply by	Divide by
Weekly	52	12
Every 2 weeks	26	12
Twice a month	24	12
Every 3 weeks	17.34	12 [1]

Add to your calculations other sources of income

(rental properties, child support, interest income). You can also use the chart above to determine the monthly income of these additional sources.

Now that you know how much money you are bringing in, it's time to decide what kind of budget you want to create. Whatever you choose, make sure that it fits your lifestyle. There are two sample budgets in Appendix B, or you may want to create your own using the samples as a guideline.

If you like detail, you may want to include all of the money-smart elements in your budget and categorize debt repayment, insurance, investments, retirement accounts. If you don't want to get that detailed, you can do a bare bones budget that will basically deduct your expenditures from your income in general categories. The sample budgets give you two extremes to work from. You may want to create something in between.

Another option for creating a budget is to use software such as Quicken or Microsoft Money. Both programs involve a learning curve in setting up the budget spread-sheets, but once the setup is complete, you can auto-matically download some of your accounts at major banks and credit card companies, which makes tracking much easier. You can also look at what you have spent in various categories and your tax-deductible expenses, and you can even project next year's spending and saving compared to next year's expected income. Keeping the program up to date is the key to making the software work for you.

If you think of the budget as your personal spending and savings plan, it will affect how you spend and save. Suddenly, you are seeing how much money you spend and finding money to save. The two

FAST FACTS:
Government figures show that many households with total income of $50,000 or less are spending more than they bring in.[2]

should go hand in hand. Your goal should be to watch your spending carefully so that you can have money to set aside—which means that the savings column of your budget should be its most exciting element. Each month, as you continue to put money in the savings category (and in the bank!), you will know that the money is growing steadily.

Creating and living with a spending and savings plan shouldn't make you feel constricted or trapped. If it does, chances are you won't stick with it. That's why the dreams you identified in Chapter 2 are so important. You will notice that on both sample budgets there is a place to identify your financial wish list, both short-term and long-term. If you are able to see what you are working toward, you will be more motivated to stick to your budget each month. Here are a few more suggestions for creating and sticking to your spending and savings plan:

- Include a category each month for "splurge money." Decide how much you can afford to spend in this category. If you know that you have money to enjoy on something frivolous each month, you will be less likely to resent the budgeting process.

- Don't pull out your budget paperwork when you are tired or frustrated. Make sure you have a positive attitude and are rested before you calculate and check your progress.

- Let other family members share the work of budgeting. You can trade months with a spouse or partner so you don't feel like you are carrying the entire load.

- Once you have several months under your belt of calculating and sticking to your budget, relax your paperwork a little. You should get into the habit of spending less and saving after you have done it for a while. There is no need to pore over your receipts and budget worksheet every week (unless you're just into that kind of thing).

- Reward yourself each month for sticking to your budget. Just make sure your reward isn't so extravagant that you bust your budget in the process!

The following chapters will walk you through how to live with your spending and savings plan so that you are able to reach your financial goals and dreams.

CASE STUDY:

Tyler and his wife, Carrie, married immediately after college. Both had jobs, and their combined income was about $95,000, which felt like a fortune to them. They were busy with work and social life, so creating a budget and living according to a spending and savings plan seemed like an unnecessary constraint. They both had several credit cards and enjoyed spending money on clothes, movies, and sushi dinners.

After a year of marriage, both Tyler and Carrie felt like their money was disappearing down a sinkhole. They couldn't afford to move out of their condo, couldn't get a decent loan on a car, and felt as if they had nothing to show for the income they were bringing in. When friends talked about how they were budgeting their money carefully, and that their projected earnings for the measly $100 a month they were plunking into an interest-bearing account were $80,000 in twenty years, Tyler and Carrie become interested. That sounded like it was worth doing, but they weren't sure if they had $100 to spare every month. In fact, they weren't sure how much they were spending, but they were determined to create a budget so they could find their extra $100 dollars to save each month.

PERSONAL REFLECTION:

Do you confuse your needs and wants? Think of examples from the past several months.

If you have never budgeted, write three reasons why. Now write three good reasons to start budgeting. Compare your lists and see which responses seem to make more sense.

YOUR TO DO LIST:

Calculate your income according to the chart above.

Now that you know how much money you have, choose a budgeting system that fits your lifestyle. Be honest about yourself: If you don't like working with numbers, will you be able to sit down with a complicated ledger sheet, or should you choose something simpler?

FOR FURTHER STUDY:

The Budget Kit
—by Judy Lawrence
The Simply Essential Personal Budgeting Kit
—by Sylvia S. Lim

CHAPTER 4

Develop Healthy Spending Habits

If you know how to spend
less than you get,
you have the philosopher's stone.

—BENJAMIN FRANKLIN

POWER STATEMENT:

Recognizing unhealthy spending habits and then replacing them with healthy spending habits allows you to "find" extra money for saving, which will help you fulfill your financial dreams and goals.

Most people wouldn't think of passing by a twenty-dollar bill if they saw it lying on the sidewalk, but people with unhealthy spending habits miss the opportunity to "find" extra money every day. They lament that they don't have any cash left over at the end of the month and can't imagine where they would get the money for investing or saving. What they don't realize is that money for investments, retirement, college tuition, and other savings is there for the taking.

If you have a financial dream, you may seriously doubt that you have any money to put toward that dream. James's wish list included a sailboat. When he was a young boy, his grandfather had taken him out and taught him to sail, but James had never been able to afford to buy his own boat. He put a timeline on his dream: In five years he wanted to have enough money for the boat. He was over halfway there. He only needed $6,000 more dollars. Could he do it in five years? Yes. Through the beauty of compounded interest, James could invest $86 a month and reach his goal. But he needed to find an additional $86 a month. There would be no other way to do it than to cut his expenses. James knew he would need an extra measure of motivation for this challenge.

Why is spending so easy, and saving so difficult? Most of us respond to the culture that surrounds us, and ours happens to encourage us to buy something even if we can't afford it. On top of that, as a culture that is frantically busy and stressed, we use consumerism for convenience, therapy, and self-esteem. Let's face it, sometimes it just feels good to buy something. But our unhealthy spending habits eventually catch up to us, and we are left with the sad reality that we haven't planned for the future or set goals to get the things we really want in life (James decided he would rather have a sailboat than three dinners out a week, trinkets for his car, and his pants dry cleaned).

When James took a close look at his spending, he identified three unhealthy habits that he had fallen into—all of which are very common.

Impulse buying

On his way home from work, James would often stop at the Farmer's Market near his house to buy something for dinner. There were several shops on his pathway to the market, and sometimes James would go inside before he picked up his dinner. He could always find something at the bookstore, and the store that sold DVDs usually had a sale going. He also found it hard to resist the temptation to head into the sporting goods store. At least once a week he saw an item he couldn't resist and he was easily able to convince himself to buy it on the spur of the moment.

Internet shopping was also an area where James practiced impulse buying. It was easy to shop from his living room with his notebook computer on his lap. Studies show that 40 percent of e-commerce purchases are made on impulse.[1] Free shipping and sale prices, as well as the ease of shopping from the comfort of your own home or office, make impulse buying on the Internet appealing, but unplanned purchases wreak havoc on anyone's budget.

Living above his means

James drove a car that he had leased, and when people saw him driving it, they assumed that he had more money than he really did. He bought nice clothes at the trendiest, most expensive stores and took golfing trips several times a year with some buddies who had more money than he did. James was a generic brand guy living in a name brand world. He was clearly living above his means and using his credit to finance his preferred lifestyle. Savings was not even on his radar.

Thomas Stanley and William Danko's book *The Millionaire Next Door* claims that three out of four millionaires drive cars more than a year old. Half of the millionaires have never spent more than $29,000 for a car or owned a wristwatch that cost more than $235.[2] On the other hand, it is not uncommon for someone with a leased

$75,000 Mercedes who takes lavish vacations to have almost no substantive wealth or investments. With today's easy credit, it's no problem to put on a façade that belies your true financial situation.

Unmonitored ATM withdrawals

James loved his debit card. Among other things, it allowed him to pull cash out of his account at a moment's notice. Some months, however, he was shocked to discover that his account was overdrawn. Even when he was trying hard to keep track of his monthly spending, he would still withdraw cash and then forget to record it. Cash was slipping through his fingers at an alarming rate as his ATM withdrawals continued to go unmonitored.

> **FAST FACTS:**
> The average consumer spends about $1,750 a year on clothing and its upkeep, according to the U.S. Bureau of Labor Statistics.[5]

If James was going to be successful at sticking to his budget and saving the money he needed for the sailboat, he was going to have to kick the unhealthy spending habits he had formed over many years. One way he motivated himself toward money-smart spending habits was to remind himself of his dream—the sailboat—then evaluate his impulse purchases in light of his goal to save enough money to buy the sailboat. When he passed the sports equipment and the electronics store on his way to get groceries, he asked himself which was more important: the sailboat or another random, unplanned purchase of running shorts and a DVD. Keeping his savings goal in front of him forced him to make important choices about spending his money.

James also did an honest assessment of his real wealth by calculating his net worth and reminding himself of that net worth number when he was tempted to spend money above his means. He realized that he had thought of his $5,000 credit card limit as part of his net worth, which gave him a false sense of his true wealth. According to financial planner Kim Dignum, incurring balances you can't pay in full is a sign you're not living within your means.[3]

James also began to take out an amount of cash each month and determined not to replenish it once it was depleted. Some financial planners suggest the envelope method—filling envelopes with cash for specified categories of spending (like entertainment, food, gas, and clothing).

One financial expert calls frugality nothing more than "creative saving."[4] It is simply the attempt to save money when you can rather than spending it. When James decided that he was going to work toward the goals that would make his financial dream a reality, he employed many methods of creative saving. Healthy spending habits transformed into savings. At the end of each month, James put a portion of his "found money" in a short-term investment account for the purchase of a sailboat.

Healthy spending habits do require a bit of creativity. Here are some additional ideas for how to "find" extra money at the end of each month:

Comparison shop. Don't be afraid to call around to get the best price on big-ticket purchases. Many stores are willing to match or lower prices to get your business from their competitors.

Eat in. Depending on the size of your family, skipping a meal out each week could result in a $160 deposit in your savings account each month. That's $1,920 a year after taxes. Make lunches instead of eating out. If you are eating out, go for the early bird specials, two-for-one dinners, and any other specials that can save you money.

Book early. Airline ticket prices are cheaper if booked thirty days in advance. Planning vacations ahead of time can save you money on airline tickets and give you time to hunt for the best deal on a hotel.

Check the thermostat. Turn down your heat in the winter and your air-conditioning in the summer. Your heating bill rises three percent for every degree you increase your thermostat over an eight-hour period. In the summer, keeping the thermostat at seventy-seven degrees will lower your bill significantly.

CASE STUDY:

Author **Judith Levine** decided one Christmas to stop buying anything but necessities for the entire upcoming year. She chronicled her experience in a book titled *Not Buying It: My Year Without Shopping*. Throughout the year, Levine made choices on what to buy based on what she determined were necessities and luxuries. Toilet paper was allowed, but cosmetics were not. Prepared or takeout food was off the list, but ingredients for making meals at home were acceptable.

The experience taught her much about the psychology of spending (she says she felt "marginalized by my nonconsumption of goods and services"), but was able to pay off an almost $8,000 credit card bill. Although she now is back to purchasing such luxuries as books and entertainment, she has all but vanquished the impulse buy. Levine now mulls clothing and other purchases overnight before buying and only buys staples when she needs them. She says that much of the medicine, toiletries, and other items she used to buy she now considers superfluous. She also found that she could live on a lot less and still be satisfied. "I had control," Levine says. "I could save money, give it away, and still have plenty of everything I wanted."

Do it yourself. Find hobbies that will keep you from having to pay someone else to do things around your house. Gardening, fixing cars, home repairs, and other do-it-yourself skills can save you big bucks.

PERSONAL REFLECTION:

How would you describe your spending habits—healthy, or unhealthy? If you are practicing any of the three unhealthy spending habits outlined above, how do you think those habits have affected your financial situation? Are you prepared to adjust your lifestyle to rid yourself of any unhealthy spending habits?

☑ YOUR TO DO LIST:

Make your own list of ways to "save creatively" according to your own lifestyle and circumstances. Start a loose change jar and empty your coins into it at the end of each day (this will also help to tidy up those countertops and couch cushions). At the end of the year, add up this found cash and use it for something you want, not something you need.

FOR FURTHER STUDY:

Your Money or Your Life: Transforming Your Relationship with Money and Achieving Financial Independence
—by Joe Dominquez

Everyday Cheapskate's Greatest Tips: 500 Simple Strategies for Smart Living
—by Mary Hunt

The Complete Tightwad Gazette
—by Amy Dacyczyn

Avoid the Debt Trap

*Never spend your money
before you have it.*

—THOMAS JEFFERSON

POWER STATEMENT:

If you know the difference
between good debt and bad
debt, you can gain money smarts
by taking advantage of good
debt and getting out from under
harmful debt.

The average American household with at least one credit card is buried under nearly $9,200 in credit card debt.[1] To make matters worse, Americans now receive five billion unsolicited credit card offers each year.[2] With the record number of personal bankruptcies and the statistics on plummeting personal savings, some financial advisors are pounding a steady drumbeat that advocates being debt-free. They offer plans for paying off all debt—starting with credit cards and ending with mortgage debt.

There are different kinds of debt, and it is important to realize that not all debt is equal. There's bad debt, and there's not-so-bad-debt. Let's start with the not-so-bad debt.

Mortgage

Most people simply cannot afford to pay cash for the purchase of a house, so they take out a loan, called a mortgage. A home is the best big-ticket purchase you will ever make, because unlike a car, a home does not begin to depreciate seconds after you have bought it. In fact, your home will continue to go up in value the longer you own it, assuming you take care of it and make improvements along the way. This also assumes that you have not taken out a mortgage that is over your head (more about money-smart house buying in Chapter 14). When April rolls around, you can deduct the interest on your mortgage from your income tax, which is another reason mortgage debt is good debt.

Student Loans

The Census Bureau did a study a few years ago and found that a college education gives you nearly double the earning potential of a high school degree. A bachelor's degree translates into $2.1 million in lifetime earnings, compared to $1.2 million for those with only a high school degree. If you have a master's degree, the earning potential goes up to $2.5 million; and if you really went all out and earned a professional degree (like an M.D. or a law degree) the potential is up to $4.4 million. The return on your investment could be up to 1,900 percent over a forty year career, according to financial planner Suze Orman.[3] The key to getting student loans repaid is simple: Just do it. Interest rates on student loans are relatively low, and lenders are willing to offer a variety of payment options. Some lenders will even be so kind as to cut big breaks to people who make their payments faithfully and on time.

Business Loans

These loans allow you to make money, and to create an asset that could appreciate over time. When it comes time to sell your business, chances are you will make money, and so the initial loan was well worth it.

Student and business loans and mortgage are necessary debt for many people. Now we turn to the not-so-good debt. Credit cards have the potential for creating bad debt, but they also can be used effectively. The key is to use them in ways that don't create debt. In other words, if you don't plan to pay off the balance each month, don't use them.

Here's why: Credit cards are unsecured debt, which means there is no asset that can be taken away if you don't pay your debt. Mortgage and car loans are secured, which means your house or your car are the collateral that the lender can take away if you don't pay. The lender has security on these kinds of loan.

FAST FACTS:

Current credit card debt in the United States totals about $360 billion.

Credit card companies don't have any security against your non-payment. So in order to offset the fact that they don't have much recourse, they charge high interest rates in the hopes that they will offset the cost of all those deadbeat cardholders.

So if you, the credit card holder, determine that you will use your credit card to live above your means and only pay the minimum amount on the bill, chances are you are getting socked with a 12, 15, or even 20 percent interest rate. Orman gives this example of how your credit card debt can hold you hostage: Assume you have a $5,000 balance on which you pay 18 percent interest, and your minimum amount due each month is 2.5 percent of the balance. If you choose to pay only the minimum amount, that works out to a payment of $125. If you make no new purchases the next month on this card (and what are the odds of that?), your minimum balance gets recomputed to a lower amount. That sounds good, except that debt amount is always recomputed to 2.5 percent each month. The bottom line is that at 2.5 percent each month, it will take you twenty-six years to get the balance down to zero if you only pay the minimum amount. And that assumes that you are putting no new charges on your card.[4]

> ## DID YOU KNOW?
>
> A recent report found that on average, people eat 83 meals out a year, and that figure climbs to about 220 if takeout meals are factored in. If the average restaurant bill is $20, then the cost of the meals out and takeout comes to about $4,400 a year. If those meals are put on a high-rate card with just the minimum monthly payments made, the net cost of the meals is about $10,000 if you factor in interest charges over the years.[7]

Credit card companies don't offer you a minimum

balance because they care about your well being. It's how they make their money. If they can keep you on the minimum balance hamster wheel every month, this guarantees that you will be handing your hard-earned money to the credit card company for years to come.

If you are already deep in debt because of your penchant for plastic, here is a plan for paying down your credit card debt from financial columnists David and Tom Gardner:

- **Stop using your cards.** Take your credit cards out of your wallet or purse and leave them at home. It's fine to keep one for emergencies, but be sure you know the difference between an emergency and an impulse buying binge.

- **Always pay more than the minimum.** Scrimp if you need to, and pay as much over the minimum as possible.

- **Plan your attack.** Pay off the card with the highest rate first, then the card with the next highest rate, and so on.

- **Reduce the interest rate.** Negotiate with your credit card company for a lower rate. Shoot for 11 or 12 percent. You'll be surprised at how many companies will lower the rate if you put a little pressure on them (tell them you are

CASE STUDY:

Anne and Damon were drowning in credit card debt. They owed over $51,000 to eight different credit card companies. Their household income is over $300,000 and they live in a nice house, drive expensive cars, and send their children to private schools. They always thought that as long as they made the minimum payments on their credit cards when they were due, this would assure that they maintained a good credit rating.

Unfortunately, they discovered that paying their credit card bills on time made up only 35 percent of their credit score. Level of debt makes up 30 percent of credit score. When the couple went to refinance their $600,000 house, their credit score was too low to qualify for a lower interest rate. So despite their high income and expensive house and cars, over 70 percent of people had a higher credit score than Anne and Damon.

A few months after they were turned down for the refinancing, the couple paid one of their monthly statements two days late. Although they had never been late before on any of their cards, half of the credit card companies jacked up the couple's rates to as high as 25 percent. Not only was their credit score plummeting, their interest rates were soaring.

Anne and Damon were caught in the debt trap, despite their luxuriant lifestyle. They decided their best course of action was to rein in their unchecked use of credit cards and get their balances down to a sane level. After they had paid off their balances, they would need to wean themselves away from perpetual credit card use and learn to live within their means.

thinking of switching to a card with a lower interest rate).

- **Consolidate your debts.** You should know what the interest rates and outstanding balances are for each of your cards, and if you have lowered the interest rate for some of them, consider combining the debt on one or more of the lower rate cards.

- **Pour any windfall into paying off your debts.** Use Christmas or birthday money, bonuses, inheritance money—any unexpected showers of money—for paying off credit card debt.[5]

Financial expert Jane Bryant Quinn suggests setting up fixed, automated monthly repayments for each of your consumer debts. For debts with low interest rates, base your payments on the current minimum due. For high-rate debts, go with slightly higher payments than you think you can afford. Programs on autopilot are far more likely to succeed than depending on your ability to make a separate decision each month, Quinn says.[6]

Some additional warnings about debt:

- Even if you are one of the savvy folks who have opted for a credit card with zero interest transfer on your balance or a low introductory interest rate, watch out for loopholes. These good deals usually have a few underlying dangers that are hidden in the fine print. For instance, if you have a low interest rate on one card and make a late payment on another card, the credit card company with the low or zero interest can find out about your late payment on the other card and then raise your rate without telling you.

- Don't spread yourself so thin on debt repayment, especially if you are determined to pay off your mortgage, that you risk not having an emergency fund or neglect to put money into a retirement account. Your mortgage payment should be the last debt you try to eliminate.

- Credit cards with rewards are great as long as they don't include an annual fee, and you don't carry any debt on the card. If you keep rolling over your debt each month, you're paying for all those airline miles or bonus points in the form of higher interest rates. Beware of the annual fees attached to these cards as well.

- Don't fall into the lure of cash advances on your credit card. If you take out a cash advance, your card company starts charging you an interest rate of 20 percent or higher. There is no grace period, and you won't be able to pay off the cash advance until you pay off the balance on your credit card.

Decide on the debt repayment system that will work

best for you. If you're reeling under a load of debt, relax, stay calm, and just take it one step at a time. You can find help at credit counseling agencies in your area. Look for nonprofits (usually supported by the United Way), and you can check an agency's history at the Better Business Bureau's website: www.bbb.org.

The most important thing is to get out of the cycle of paying for things with credit and then carrying over a balance on that debt. Once you are free of the debt trap, you will be ready to channel your money into places where it can really work for you.

PERSONAL REFLECTION:

Are you living above your means by using credit cards to pay for things you can't afford? When was the last time you actually paid cash (green treasury bills) for something? Have you gotten so used to using credit cards that you have lost touch with the value of money?

YOUR TO DO LIST:

Add up all the money you spend each month on credit card payments, then think about what you could do with that amount of money if you weren't giving it to the credit card companies. Write down a plan to tackle your debt, using the suggestions in this chapter. Commit to stick to the plan until you have paid off your credit card debt.

FOR FURTHER STUDY:

Generation Debt: Take Control of Your Money: A How-To Guide
—by Carmen Wong Ulrich

Credit Card Nation: The Consequences of America's Addiction to Credit
—by Robert D. Manning

Good Debt, Bad Debt: Knowing the Difference Can Save Your Financial Life
—by Jon Hanson

CHAPTER 6

Cultivate a Savings Mentality

If you would be wealthy,
think of saving as well as getting.
—BENJAMIN FRANKLIN

POWER STATEMENT:

Saving is an important part of a healthy financial future and setting aside money for funds, especially an emergency cushion fund, should be a part of every budget.

Remember piggy banks? They were usually pink and would sit prominently on a child's dresser or desk, collecting coins and perhaps a few paper bills. The idea was simple: spend a little, save a little. In the bottom of the piggy bank was a little stopper that could be pulled out whenever the child wanted to raid his savings fund. A frugal child would have a heavy pig. A spendthrift child would only hear a couple of coins clinking around in his pig.

Today, adults have a similar kind of piggy bank in a variety of choices—401(k) accounts, money market mutual funds, certificates of deposit, savings accounts—with one major difference: These accounts actually multiply your money. If you put $100 every month in a piggy bank and save it for a rainy day, when the rainy day arrives three years later you have exactly $3,600. If you put $100 every month in an interest bearing account that earns 2 percent a year, the rainy day fund will be $3,714. We'll talk more about investing in Part Two of this book. The goal of this chapter is to get you thinking about the benefits of saving your money.

According to recent findings by the U.S. Commerce Department, Americans prefer spending over saving. In January of 2006, the personal savings rate fell into negative territory at minus 0.5 percent. The savings rate has been negative for an entire year only twice before, in 1932 and 1933, when Americans had to deplete their savings to cope with overwhelming job losses and business failures caused by the Great Depression.[1]

In 1984, the savings rate was 10.8 percent, and has been declining steadily since. According to Nancy Register of the Consumer Federation of America, the culture and habit of savings has been lost over the past two generations. The marketing pressure to spend and buy is prevalent, says Register, and the attitude is that if you can't buy it now, put it on your credit card.[2]

Consumers are hit with temptations to buy and accumulate, but there isn't much effort to market savings. After all, it's much easier to convince someone that they need the latest electronic gadget than it is to convince them to sock that money away for the future. Spending just seems like more fun—that is, until you run smack into one of those rainy days.

Here are four reasons to cultivate a savings mentality:

Life is full of unexpected financial surprises. Ideally, you should have a cash fund that is equal to at least six months' living costs plus expenses (this is bare bones expenses and doesn't include weekly manicures or four nights out on the town). You never know when your car may break down or your company might downsize, and if you don't have a cushion fund, you will be reduced to pulling out your credit card and running up an ugly balance. Your cushion fund can be built up gradually. Make it a goal to get the equivalent of one month's salary under your belt, then keep up your savings mentality for another few months. Keep funding your cushion account until you have at least four months, then move on to funding other accounts.

This money should go into an account that is liquid, which means you can get your hands on the cash quickly. A bank money market deposit account is a federally insured account that is easy to start (just ask your bank to open one for you). You're limited to about six transfers or withdrawals a month, three of which can be with a personal check or your debit card. You could also put your cushion fund in a money market mutual fund, which works much like a bank account. If you own other mutual funds, it's easy to add another fund to the account. You can deposit cash, earn interest, and withdraw the money at any time. The interest rates change daily,

FAST FACTS:

According to a recent poll, 53 percent of Americans claim they cannot afford to save, yet 58 percent of those polled treat themselves to movies and restaurant meals regularly.[4]

depending on the rates in the open market, and the rates are usually a bit higher than those offered by banks.

You should keep your cushion fund separate from other accounts.[3] Even if it costs a little more to keep more than one savings account, it's worth it if it keeps you from dipping into the account for things like vacations and holiday gift giving. If you can't muster the discipline to fund your cushion fund each month, have the specified amount automatically deducted from your paycheck each month. Any bonuses or cash gifts you get should also be applied to your fund until it is built up.

Savings can cover those "now and then" expenses. These include insurance premiums, property taxes, and holiday and birthday gifts. These are expenses that come up every year, but not monthly. When you are trying to budget, it's easy to overlook these expenses. When it's time to pay them, if you're not prepared, out comes the credit card once again. A short-term account for these kinds of expenses will keep you from resorting to credit. A good place to keep this money would be in a bank's passbook savings account, which is almost as good as a checking account in terms of liquidity. You won't get much of a return on this money, but if you are going to be using it within the year, you will need to put it somewhere out of reach, yet easily accessible.

You have dreams that you want to fulfill in the next twelve to twenty-four months. You may have your eye on a leather couch and chair for the den. Instead of buying it right now and running up your credit card bill (if you don't have the money to pay cash for it this month, chances are you won't next month either), you can use the money that you have been faithfully stashing away in your short-term accounts. If you have made a list of your short-term and long-term financial dreams, then you already have something that you can be saving for. It is much more gratifying to wait until you have the money saved and can pay cash for it instead of getting it now and adding to your debt.

DID YOU KNOW?

If you are getting a tax refund each year, you are withholding too much money from your paycheck, and are simply getting repaid your own money. If you change your withholding so that less money is subtracted from your paycheck, you will have more money to pay your bills on time and to set aside money for savings each month. You can calculate how much you should withhold on **www.suzeorman.com.** It will help you determine how to fill out your W-4 form so that you don't withhold too much money (and end up owing the IRS money at tax time).[5]

You have dreams that you want to fulfill ten years or more down the road. Everyone should have a big financial dream that they are working toward. It may be as simple as retiring at fifty-five, or it may be a grandiose dream of buying an Italian villa. We'll discuss where to put this money in Chapter 11. Whatever it is, you will have to plan for it by saving money. If you count on the money appearing at the time you have decided to fulfill your dream, then you really are dreaming.

A saving mentality means that you will often have to delay gratification and discipline yourself to live within a budget. Although neither of those sounds very appealing at the outset, once you have begun saving your money and watching it grow, the process gets more enticing.

Julia, who was used to buying things she wanted on credit and never budgeting, worked for a company that changed ownership, then talked about layoffs. She began to worry, and so she decided to meet with a financial planner, who set up two accounts for her. One account was a cushion fund where she would deposit a small amount of money each month in case her company decided to follow through with layoffs. The other account was for additional expenses that might come along in the next couple of years, including any short-term financial goals she decided to set. The planner also encouraged Julia to take advantage of her company's 401(k) matching fund so that she could begin to prepare for retirement.

The savings mentality didn't come immediately for Julia. She had to find ways to cut back her rampant spending and credit card dependency. Although each month her take-home pay was enough to include adding money to these funds, she had been used to impulse buying and cash flow ignorance. She found ways to develop healthy spending habits and rediscover the money that had been slipping through her fingers each month. Julia decided to automate her savings account payments so she didn't have to decide each month whether to put money back or spend it on dinners out and mall shopping sprees. Her budget was now adjusted, and the money for savings was out of the picture. She learned to live without it, and was satisfied in knowing that it was growing a little each month. Now that she was in the habit of spending less and saving more, it was easier for Julia to live within her budget.

A savings mentality is directly tied to understanding your net worth, cash flow, and identifying your financial dreams and goals. Julia decided that it was more important to set and work toward short-term and long-term financial goals than to indulge in living beyond her means. As she watched her savings and investments grow, she realized that she was paving the way for a future without sleepless nights worrying over her finances.

PERSONAL REFLECTION:

Do you have enough money each month to put into a savings or investment account? If the answer is no, is it because you are living above your means?

Do you have a cushion fund? If not, what plan do you have in place in the event of a financial emergency?

☑ YOUR TO DO LIST:

If you don't have a cushion fund, calculate three months' salary plus living expenses and make a goal of depositing a small amount of money in a savings account each month until you have built up this fund.

Look for ways that you can cut out expensive non-essentials to gather more money for saving (like wash more and dry clean less, take public transportation, stay home for the movies, or cook at home instead of eating out).

FOR FURTHER STUDY:

Saving on a Shoestring: How to Cut Expenses, Reduce Debt and Stash More Cash
—by Barbara O'Neill

Yankee Magazine's *Living Well on a Shoestring: 1,501 Ingenious Ways to Spend Less for What You Need and Have More for What You Want,* Yankee Magazine

50 Simple Things You Can Do to Improve Your Personal Finances: How to Spend Less, Save More, and Make the Most of What You Have
—by Ilyce Glink

CHAPTER **7**

Spend
Savvy

---

*It is an unfortunate human failing
that a full pocketbook often groans more loudly
than an empty stomach.*

—FRANKLIN DELANO ROOSEVELT

POWER STATEMENT:

Major purchases should be made
with careful thought and planning
to avoid jeopardizing your financial
dreams and goals.

There's one quick way to bust your budget and crash your financial goals and dreams: make a big purchase. There is nothing wrong with buying a boat, or a car, or a plasma television, but if you make these purchases without a plan, you could make a big mistake that will cost you money now and in the future. The seductive lure of those big ticket items have caused well-intentioned budgeters to abandon their money smarts and plunge into debt, which sets them back further in reaching their goals.

Maria had been keeping a budget for several months because she wanted to save money for a cruise when she finished her MBA. She had kept tight rein on her spending, given her credit cards a reprieve, and put money into a savings account each month. Things were going well until she began to see car advertisements for dealer incentives. She thought it might be a good time to get a new car, since her old green sedan had seen better days. After all, she was doing so well on her budget and saving money, and with the good deals the car dealerships were offering, how could she go wrong?

What Maria didn't realize is that she could go wrong in several different ways. She needed to give careful thought to the decision she was about to make instead of leaping hastily into the treacherous waters of car buying.

Big purchases are especially dangerous when they are

made on impulse. Advertisements for auto dealer incentives, six months same as cash, no-tax weekends, and other deals that are too good to pass up can tempt the consumer into making quick purchases that haven't been thoroughly researched, well thought out, and planned. Here are suggestions for using money smarts when purchasing those big ticket items.

Buying a Car

The first step in planning for the purchase of a car is to decide if you really need a new car. The moment you drive a brand new car off the lot, it begins to depreciate, so you need to think carefully about this purchase. Is your old car in need of repairs? According to financial consultant Peter Sander, a $1,500 car repair could equal the transaction costs of a new car in many states.[1] By the time you pay sales tax, registration fees, and the difference in insurance premiums, you could have repairs done on the car you're driving and save yourself quite a bit of money.

There are good reasons to trade in your old car for a new one. If your family structure changes (you have three kids and another one on the way), you will need to find a vehicle with more seatbelts, leg room, and cup holders. You may also determine that your old clunker is unsafe and beyond repair. If, after careful evaluation and thought, you determine that you are in need of a car, the next decision you will need to make is whether to buy or lease.

Leasing a car makes sense if your work situation demands that you have a new car every two or three years. If, however, you are looking to make smart money choices and you don't have to have a new car every time next year's models roll off the assembly line, then you should pass on the lease. Here's why. At the end of your lease contract, you will have three choices: buy the car at a pre-negotiated price, which is usually higher than the value of the car; buy another car; or lease another car. Most people choose to lease another car, and start three more years of monthly car payments, which is money that could be eventually going into savings and investments.

Leasing companies also will charge you extra when you turn in the car if you have dents, or even car dings in the doors. You can also be charged for wear and tear and mileage over your limit. If you take vacations and lose track of your mileage, fifteen cents for every mile over your 12,000 limit can add up.

If you opt to buy a car, here are a few money-smart suggestions:

- Consider a used car. Because cars depreciate so quickly, you can get a certified pre-owned (CPO) car with low mileage and a dealer warranty. Many of these cars are only a year or two old and are certified by the manufacturer, which means you won't get stuck with somebody's else's clunker.

- Shop around for a good loan, since the dealer doesn't always offer the best deal. Check your local bank or credit union or websites like www.lendingtree.com or www.eloan.com. Do this legwork before you walk into the dealership.

- If you are buying a new car, negotiate a price that is close to the invoice price listed on the sticker. You should also be aware that there is a holdback price that the dealer sends the manufacturer, as well as some factory-to-dealer incentives that make the dealer a good chunk of change. It's worth it to do a little research so that you can negotiate a price that makes the dealer a little money and keeps you from getting the bad end of the deal. Good websites for researching this include: www.edmunds.com, www.autobytel.com, www.autoweb.com, and www.thecarconnection.com.

- Financial consultant Suze Orman suggests that during the negotiating process, you ask for the "out-the-door" price, which is insider lingo for the price minus all those hidden costs that will turn up on your paperwork.[2]

- Talk about financing deals after you have negotiated your buying price, not during the process. If you have already done research

> on your own, you will be knowledgeable
> and equipped to compare the dealer's
> financing with other financing options.

For other big ticket purchases, such as boats, home remodeling, kitchen appliances, or the fancy plasma television, Peter Sander offers this advice: Build a savings component into your budget and set aside funds off the top of your income. The funds can be separated into a different account, or remain a designated portion of your primary savings account. If the need arises quickly (like the refrigerator that can't be resurrected), or if there is a big price break, purchasing on credit is permissible if it is carefully planned. You should calculate the monthly payment of the item and put it in the budget, but be sure the overall purchase cost will be lower when you calculate in the cost of the credit. You don't want to use sale prices as a rationale for busting your budget.

Purchase extended warranties selectively. According to *Consumer Reports* magazine, they can make sense on certain items such as exercise equipment, laptop computers, and plasma televisions. These items have greater odds of needing repairs within three years, and most standard warranties are for only a year or less. For other items, however, the odds are much lower that you will collect on extended warranties. The retailers make big money from selling extended warranties, so be careful about falling for the sales pitch.[3]

Avoid falling into the trap of thinking you must have the big ticket item now. Unless you have an appliance that has suddenly conked out or the laser printer you have been eyeing is on close-out special, plan your purchase well ahead of time so that you can save up the money and pay cash. You will feel better if you haven't succumbed to the "buy now, pay later" mentality. If you have not taken care of your other financial needs—cushion fund, college and retirement accounts on track, debt under control—

DID YOU KNOW?

The moment you drive a new car off the lot, it loses about 20 percent of its value; within three years, its value will decline by at least one-third. If you pay $20,000 for a new car, after two years of driving, it might be worth $13,000. That's $3,500 of depreciation costs a year—almost $300 a month.[4]

then you should reconsider any kind of luxury purchase.

If you have developed a savings mentality, you may already have the funds available in an account you have set up for just this kind of purchase. Some purchases require additional costs to maintain—boats, swimming pools, dirt bikes. These maintenance costs should be evaluated carefully as well. If you are dipping into a savings account to put in a pool, have you considered the cost of cleaning, repairing, and maintaining the pool? Buying a big ticket item without carefully considering all the additional costs of the item could lead to financial problems that linger long past the moment of purchase.

CASE STUDY:

Maria had a good credit (FICO) score and was able to qualify for the zero percent financing that the car dealer was offering; however, the dealer was also offering $3,000 cash back. She was unsure which deal was the best. With zero percent interest, the $19,500 car she was considering would be payments of $325 for 60 months. If she took the $3,000 cash back, she would reduce her price to $16,500. With her attractive FICO score, she could qualify for a good interest rate, perhaps somewhere around 6.0 percent, which works out to payments of $319 a month, or $6 less.

Maria didn't think that sounded like enough money to worry over, but when she did the math she realized that over the life of the loan, it added up to $360. If the car had been over $20,000 she would have been better off taking the zero percent interest. The more expensive the car, the more she would end up saving by going for the zero percent financing deal.

PERSONAL REFLECTION:

Think about a big ticket items that you purchased without careful evaluation and planning. How did this purchase affect you financially? Did you incur more debt?

Do you find yourself impatient about making large purchases, or are you willing to wait until you have money saved for them?

YOUR TO DO LIST:

Write down one big ticket item that you are likely to purchase without careful planning in the next two months.

Write down a plan for purchasing this item:

- Evaluate the need.
- Determine the cost, the timing, and what kind of return you can get on your savings.
- Now break the goal into monthly savings goals.

FOR FURTHER STUDY:

Edmunds.com Strategies for Smart Car Buyers
   —by Philip Reed

Buying Cars Without Buying the Farm!
   —by Maxwell Stone

Get Insurance for Assurance

The typical worker spends more time making breakfast than choosing a health plan.

—LESLIE HAGGIN GEARY, MONEY MAGAZINE

POWER STATEMENT:

A car accident, home accident or illness can wipe out your cushion fund, investments and home equity, so it is important to have money smarts about buying and maintaining insurance.

Life has a way of getting complicated. Financial columnist and author Jane Brant Quinn compares insurance to a safety net that will catch us when something catastrophic such as fire, accident, sickness, or premature death leave us dangling precariously from the high wire. It only takes one slip to send us plummeting to the ground with all our financial assets falling along with us. Insurance is the net that catches us and puts us back into action so that we can get on with life.

Buying insurance can also get complicated. If you are not careful, you could end up spending more money and getting less coverage than you need. What kinds of insurance do you need? Here is a quick list:

- Homeowner's
- Auto
- Health
- Disability
- Long-term care

Here is insurance you might need:

- Life (if you have dependents)
- Liability

Following is a quick primer in weaving your way through the insurance maze.

Homeowner's Insurance. If you are still paying on your mortgage loan, chances are you're required to have this insurance. One of the best money-smart moves you can make with mortgage insurance is to look at combining this policy and your auto policy.

You should insure for as much as you can, since your home is likely to be your biggest financial asset. Annual premiums, however, can be costly—$1,000 or more in some areas. For families on a budget, this can be a real strain. If you are willing to raise your deductible, then your premium will go down. A deductible of $500, $1,000, or even $5,000 can lower your premium by 30 to 40 percent. The key is to have money set back in your cushion fund to offset the cost if you should have to pay on your deductible.

A "replacement cost" policy will cover the cost of rebuilding your house if it burns to the ground. The policy also increases every year in line with construction costs. A word of warning: Don't tie the size of your insurance policy to the resale value of your house. That value includes land, which can't be insured. The cost to repair or rebuild has nothing to do with what a buyer might offer you for your house.

Most policies don't cover floods and earthquakes. You have to get a special rider or separate insurance, and you should definitely do so if you live in an area prone to these kinds of disasters.

Auto Insurance. If you have a computer and access to the Internet, you can shop 'til you drop for auto insurance. And you should. A company with a low cost quote can save you hundreds of dollars a year. According to Quinn, when deciding on a policy, you need to be sure it includes 1) a hefty amount of liability coverage; 2) zero or minimal medical-payments coverage if you already have health insurance; 3) collision insurance for accidents, and if your car is a new model, comprehensive insurance to cover

DID YOU KNOW?

Members of the American Automobile Association (AAA) collectively save more than $27 million annually on their auto insurance just by providing their membership information when they purchase a policy.[5]

random damage and theft. If you have an older-model car worth less than $2,000, you'll probably pay more for the coverage than you would ever collect on a claim; and 4) a significant amount of uninsured and underinsured motorist coverage, in case you're injured or disabled by a hit-and-run or someone with no or insufficient coverage.[1]

You can also save money on your auto insurance by taking advantage of low-mileage discounts. You should also ask about discounts for antilock brakes, airbags, and other safety features. It may sound strange, but driving safely is a good way to protect your money. Although your insurance company can't suddenly cancel your policy, they can refuse to renew it, which will leave you driving around without a much-needed safety net.

Health Insurance. There isn't room in this chapter to discuss all facets of the complicated world of health insurance, so we'll only discuss ways to help keep your health insurance costs down. We list a few in-depth resources about health care coverage at the end of this chapter. Whether you are insured by an individual or employee covered health plan, you can keep costs down by raising your deductible and co-payments on both care services and prescription drugs.

The coverage offered by HMOs (health maintenance organizations) can be less expensive and is good for young families that need routine care; however, you are restricted to doctors and hospitals that fall within the plan. PPOs (preferred provider organizations) offer you the opportunity to see specialists and get medical tests without referrals, as well as more control over your care, but you pay higher premiums and co-pays. Catastrophic coverage allows you to pay all your medical bills up to a certain ceiling—$2,000, $5,000, or $10,000—and the insurer covers the rest. This coverage is preferable if you can't afford a comprehensive plan but want to protect yourself from a financial disaster due to health costs.

If you are covered by a company health plan and have access to a flexible spending account, you can cut medical costs by 15 to 35 percent. Your company will deduct a fixed amount from each paycheck and then deposit it into a personal account—the amount is up to you, but the maximum is usually $3,000 to $5,000 a year. You will then use the money from that account to pay for medical and dental bills that your insurance doesn't cover; however, you must spend all the money deposited by a certain date or the leftover cash goes back to the company. A flexible spending account is usually a good way to save money on health costs.

If you don't have a company health plan, and you are buying individual health insurance, consider buying high-deductible catastrophic coverage. Even though you have to pay the smaller bills out of your own pocket, you are covered for serious illnesses. Another option if you're self-employed is a health savings account (HSA). It works this way: You make a tax-deductible contribution each year to the account, and pay the medical bills out of the account, tax-free. You choose a deductible that you are willing to pay each year, typically $1,000 to $5,000 for an individual and $5,000 to $10,000 for a family. The insurer pays most of the bills over that amount.

An HSA combines the high-deductible catastrophic health insurance with a tax-favored savings plan. This plan is best if you're rarely sick and can build up large financial reserves, or if you have enough money to pay medical bills from your income and can treat the HSA like a tax-deferred retirement account. For self-employed people, an HSA offers a bonus: You can accumulate the money you don't use from year to year, and in some plans you can channel it into mutual funds and take it out at retirement under the same rules as other retirement funds.

Disability Insurance. No one anticipates being too sick to work, but there is a one-in-three chance that a twenty-year-old worker will become disabled before retirement age. In fact, before age sixty-five, you're more likely to become disabled than to die.[2] If you do not have a policy through your employer and are shopping policies, here's what to look for:

- The percentage of income replaced should be between 60 and 80 percent (if you are covered by your employer, check the policy). If you can afford the higher cost, go for 80 percent income replaced.

- The coverage should be up to sixty-five years of age.

- Coverage should include mental illness, stress disorders, back pain, severe migraines, and other common maladies that keep people from working.

- If possible, make sure that commissions, bonuses, and overtime are a part of the income to be replaced, especially if you depend on these.

Even if you don't have dependents, you should have disability insurance. You still have to take care of yourself in the event of a debilitating illness.

Long-Term Care Insurance. An often overlooked insurance plan is the one that will keep you from using all your savings and investment money to fund your nursing home or constant care facility. If you're married, long-term care insurance keeps your spouse from using all the savings for long-term medical costs and having nothing left to live on. If you're middle income or below, the premiums for long-term care insurance may be more than you can afford, but these policies are cheaper to buy when you are young. Be careful, however, not to ignore your retirement accounts and college tuition funds. Those should be priorities.

> **FAST FACTS:**
>
> An average couple retiring this year will need $200,000 to cover their healthcare costs for twenty years in retirement, not including the expense of long-term care.[4]

Find out what nursing homes cost, and decide whether you want to insure for the full amount or for less and pay the difference out of savings. Pick a waiting period before payments kick in (a policy with a six-month wait costs less than one with a three-month wait) and insure for the longest period you can afford, typically three to five years.

Life Insurance. If you have dependents, you need life insurance. If you die early, expenses will still go on, and your family will need the safety net of life insurance. The least expensive type of policy is term life insurance. This kind of policy assures that your family will be taken care of for a certain amount of time (term). The term you choose should take into account how long you need to provide protection. If you are buying the policy to take care of your children, then you will probably want coverage until your youngest child is through college, so you should choose a policy with a term that will cover that. If your child is five, a twenty-year policy would do.

A cash-value policy can carry a premium five times the cost of term insurance or more, and the policy is in place for the rest of your life. That means that the insurance company could easily collect three times more from the premiums you pay than they will pay out in the death benefit. Financial writer Marshall Brain gives this example: If you wanted to purchase $100,000 of life insurance as a term policy, you might pay $15 each month. If you bought it as a cash-value policy, you might pay $100 a month. Depending on the company selling the policy, you will then be assured that the difference ($85 a month) will act as an investment that will pay off the life insurance and/or pay you a cash-value at age sixty-five. The problem, Brain says, is that the savings part of this kind of policy is inefficient. You would be much better off simply depositing the $85 in a stock mutual fund each month.[3]

When choosing between a term life insurance policy and a cash-value policy, watch the pros and cons. Term life insurance is affordable and reliable; but the premium goes up periodically, and the policy may be canceled at age sixty-five or seventy, paying no dividends and having no cash value. A cash-value policy, on the other hand, is more expensive and offers less coverage; but at a certain point, the policy is "paid up" and accumulates cash value, interest, and dividends (if purchased from a mortgage company), and the policy extends as long as you live. As a couple other pluses, the premium on a cash-value policy will never be raised, and you may "dip in" or cash in the policy if a financial need arises.

Obviously, there are pluses and minuses to both types of policy, and different experts have different feelings on each. One option to consider is buying a cash-value policy with a "term insurance rider," which enables the buyer to get the best of both worlds.

Insurance may seem a little like gambling—except with this type of gambling, you hope that there is no big payout. Keep in mind, however, that living without insurance is an even bigger financial gamble.

PERSONAL REFLECTION:

Are you gambling without insurance in any of the areas listed in this chapter? If you have insurance, are you knowledgeable about all your policies and are you confident you are getting the best deal for your money?

☑ YOUR TO DO LIST:

If you are lacking insurance in any of the areas above, research the cost of buying a policy and compare it with the money that you would lose if something catastrophic occurred. If you have insurance in all of the areas listed in this chapter, review your policies to see if you are covered adequately and that you aren't paying more than you should.

FOR FURTHER STUDY:

The New Health Insurance Solution: How to Get Cheaper, Better Coverage Without a Traditional Employer Plan
—by Paul Zane Pilzer

Hassle-Free Health Care Coverage: How to Buy the Right Medical Insurance Cheaply and Effectively
—by Merritt Publishing

New Life Insurance Investment Advisor: Achieving Financial Security for You and Your Family Through Today's Insurance Products
—by Ben Baldwin

CHAPTER 9

Make Finances a Family Affair

A family solves difficult problems everyday.
Money is just one of them.

—TERRY RIGGS

POWER STATEMENT:

Making money decisions together and teaching children about financial literacy are important elements for the money smart family.

L ove and money can be a dangerous combination. According to a recent poll, 84 percent of husbands and wives admit that money is a source of tension in their marriage, and many parents are more comfortable talking to their teenagers about sex than about their income.[1] Money can often create a wall in family relationships that causes spouses, parents, children, and extended family members to make unwise money decisions.

Glenda and Patrick, a young engaged couple, talked openly about almost everything before they married. They planned how they would divide the household responsibilities and when they would begin a family; they even talked about where they wanted to retire. But they never talked about money, despite their very different money personalities (Patrick was thrifty and Glenda loved to spend). They brought into their marriage a code of silence when it came to money, which made them unable to sit down and talk about how they would spend, save, and invest. Their finances were unorganized and there were no goals and dreams that they were working toward together.

Psychologists agree that money plays an important role in family relationships—from marriage to parenting. Communication, honesty, education, and planning can go a long way in solving the money conflicts within families.

Before Marriage

In a marriage counseling session, Amy and Vince were surprised to find that the counselor spent a remarkable amount of time talking with them about money issues. They knew that money was a big stress factor in many marriages, but they had assumed that when money problems arose after the nuptials, they would just deal with them.

The counselor, however, warned against waiting until they were married to deal with potential riffs about money. Instead, she encouraged them to spend several sessions discussing their money personalities, habits, and debt. In the course of their discussion, the couple realized that they had some very different ideas about how they should spend their money. Getting these issues out in the open before the marriage would spare them the heartache of trying to iron out these touchy financial issues while juggling a new baby, jobs, and the additional stresses of married life.

For one thing, Amy discovered that Vince had quite a bit of debt that she didn't know about. For now, it was Vince's problem. But after the wedding ceremony, the debt would become Amy's problem also.

According to financial author Deborah Knuckey, if either person is bringing financial baggage into the relationship—credit card debt or a bad FICO score—they should vow to clean it up as soon as possible. What begins as the single person's financial problem becomes the married couple's problem, and can potentially bring even more stress into the newlywed relationship.[2]

Engaged couples should start a dialogue about long-term financial planning. Although those plans may need to be adjusted after marriage, beginning the discussion allows couples to gain knowledge about the future spouse's money attitudes and priorities. Once couples understand the other person's financial personality, they can set parameters and roles for the relationship, such as whether they will share a bank account and what is a reasonable spending budget.

After Marriage

Whatever you do, it's better if you do it together. Whether it is budgeting, investing, paying off debt, or just finding ways to save money, couples need to come together and share the load. This will involve ongoing communication about finances. If the wife isn't privy to investment information, she may be at a disadvantage when it comes to making decisions. According to a *Money* magazine survey, 73 percent of husbands claim to be responsible for investment decisions, while 57 percent of wives do the budgeting.[3]

Even if the husband handles the investments and the wife handles the budgeting, both spouses should have full knowledge of what is going on in each of these areas. Arguments can flare up when financial roles are divided. For example, let's say one husband does all of the investment and long-term planning, while the wife

> ### DID YOU KNOW?
>
> Collectively, teens spend more than $100 billion annually on clothes, entertainment, and food, but 60 percent of teens cannot explain the difference between cash, checks, and credit cards.[7]

does all the day-to-day spending (kids' clothes, household items, groceries). She may also do the budgeting, but the husband isn't really in on the budgeting or the daily spending.

When he perceives that she spends too much money on something, he may blow up and accuse her of not caring about the family's finances. While this may not be true, if she isn't in on the long-term plan of saving for retirement or their child's college fund, she may not understand that he's interested in saving as much money as possible for these long-term funds. He, on the other hand, doesn't have much idea of how much things cost and how difficult it is to try and stick with a budget when cereal costs $4.50 a box and the kids outgrow their clothes every three months. If this couple were to sit down together and talk about the investment plans and the daily budget, they would be able to work together to stay within the budget and save for long-term investments.

According to financial consultant Dave Ramsey, it will be much easier to reach goals if both spouses are on board and equally determined to succeed.[4] Spouses should also know what they've got and where it is. Wives should know what money exists in which account, and husbands should know how much money is in the checking account. There should be no mysteries. According to financial consultants, couples with no money secrets are those with the best chance of surviving financial challenges that will come up throughout the years of marriage.

After Kids

It's never too early to start training children to respect money. According to the Jump$tart Coalition for Personal Financial Literacy, the average student who graduates from high school lacks basic skills in the management of personal financial affairs. Many are unable to balance a checkbook and most simply have no insight into the basic survival principles involved with earning, spending, saving, and investing.[5]

What age should parents start teaching their children about money? Financial experts agree that it's never too early. The more children know about money, the better they will be at making wise financial decisions as they grow older.

A generation ago, children were taught the basics about finances—mortgages, compounded interest, and the Federal Reserve—in home economics classes. Today, those classes have mostly disappeared, and children are rarely taught financial literacy in school. The most critical lessons of financial literacy are best taught at home, however. Here are a few things parents can do to make sure their children have money smarts:

- Teach young children how to count money. Practice simple games like placing a nickel on the left side of the table and five pennies on the right. Continue the strategy using dimes, quarters, and half dollars.

- Teach them to save. Have children set aside part of their allowance for something they really want, while still keeping money available for treats and movies. This teaches them the value of both short-term and long-term saving.

- Teach your children how to make money. Help them brainstorm ways they can earn money by doing jobs that are suitable for their age.

CASE STUDY:

Jill and Daniel decided that they didn't want their son, Justin, to repeat the financial mistakes they had made in their young adult years. Neither had been taught fiscal responsibility growing up, and they entered marriage deep in credit card debt. It was a stress on their marriage, and only when they decided to work together to create a financial plan did they begin to realize the importance of money smarts.

They wanted Justin to have money smarts long before he was out on his own, so they came up with a plan to help him become financially literate. They started by giving him a small allowance when he was five years old and helping him decide how to spend the allowance. They taught him how to count money so he would know how much money he had. When he spent his week's allowance on something the first day and didn't have any money for the rest of the week, they used the experience as a lesson about how to save and spend wisely.

As he grew older, they increased the amount of his allowance each year and opened a small savings account for him at age ten. By this time, he had learned the value of saving money, and so he began to put a portion of his allowance, some of this birthday and Christmas money, and some of the money he earned from doing chores for neighbors into his account.

When Justin was fifteen, his parents helped him make a spending plan. He was now working after school and Saturdays at the local hardware store, so he was bringing in more money. He calculated his expected income (job, allowance, gifts and other sources), then identified a long-term goal. He then figured out how much he would need to save each week to reach his goal, and how much money he could spend.

Jill and Daniel also taught Justin how to balance a checkbook; how to make deposits and withdrawals from an ATM machine; how to do grocery shopping, including writing the list, checking sale ads, and making purchases within a pre-determined budget; and how to manage a credit card account. By the time Justin left for college, he was financially literate, and able to make money-smart decisions.

- Enroll pre-teens in a financial course suited for their age. Check your local library or bank information about courses.

- Be a good role model. Most high schoolers say they learn "everything they need to know about money" from their parents. If you want your child to be smart with money, then you must set the standard. A survey conducted by Northwestern Mutual Financial Network revealed that only 25 percent of Americans save anything at all on a monthly basis for long-term goals, and 50 percent of Americans are not paying off credit cards each month.[6] Don't let your financial behavior set a poor standard for your children.

PERSONAL REFLECTION:

If you are married, do you and your spouse have open communication about finances? Do you have a plan for your finances that the two of you have worked out together?

Are you a good role model for teaching your children money smarts? If not, in what areas do you need to improve?

✓ YOUR TO DO LIST:

If you are married, sit down with your spouse and make sure the two of you understand the family finances. If you each handle different roles in money management, keep each other informed of what is happening in those areas (i.e., budgeting, investing, saving).

If you have children, read up on ways to teach them about money and start putting some practical literacy tools into place. A few options are listed below under "For Further Study."

FOR FURTHER STUDY:

Teaching Kids About Money: Cool Tools for Training Tomorrow's Millionaires
—by Dave Ramsey

Teen Money Tips: Simple Steps for Banking, Saving and Making Money
—by Sanyika Calloway Boyce

The Young Couples' Guide to Growing Rich Together
—by Jill Gianola

Conscious Spending for Couples: Seven Skills for Financial Harmony
   —by Deborah Knuckey

Smart Couples Finish Rich: 9 Steps to Creating a Rich Future for You and Your Partner
   —by David Bach

PART II

INVESTING

Understanding the Value of Investing

Never invest your money
in anything that eats or needs repairing.
—BILLY ROSE

POWER STATEMENT:

Understanding the importance and value of investing will help you make wise decisions about where to put your money.

What does it take to be a millionaire? A huge inheritance might nudge you toward the seven-figure rank, and winning the lottery would get you there in a flash. Most people, however, aren't going to achieve one of these quick-cash ways to millionaire status, and so they must opt for something else. So how can you make a million dollars?

Here's one way: Let's assume that at age twenty-five you start investing $440 a month at an interest rate of 10 percent. In thirty years you will have accumulated somewhere in the neighborhood of $1,011,000.[1]

Here's another example: Bill and Eve are both twenty-two years old but they have very different attitudes about money. Eve wants to invest some money, so she scrapes together $2,000 a year to invest. Her growth rate is 9 percent. She does this for only nine years, however and stops after investing a total of $18,000.

Bill doesn't want to invest at such a young age, and so he doesn't begin putting money back until he's thirty-two. He also invests $2,000 a year, but he continues putting his money into the account for thirty-two years. In total, he invests $70,000 at a 9 percent growth rate. At age sixty-five, Bill has now earned $470,249 in his investment account. Not bad. Eve, however, now has $579,471, even though she stopped investing thirty-two years earlier! The lesson: The earlier you understand the value of investing, the more time your money has to grow.

Financial advisors Tom and Dave Gardner define investing as putting your money "into some form of 'security'—a fancy word for anything that is 'secured' by some assets. Stocks, bonds, mutual funds, certificates of deposit—all these are types of securities."[2] Investing creates wealth. It's a simple fact, but one that many people overlook. They believe that investing is complicated, and only for the already-wealthy. Nothing could be further from the truth. Here are a few more myths that keep people from investing:

You need a financial planner.

They used to be called stockbrokers, but now they're financial planners, consultants, or advisors. Whatever they're called, you should tread carefully when deciding whether to hire one. Many brokers are simply salespeople at heart and their goal is to seal the deal. They don't have the same respect for and attachment to your money that you do. A good broker will try to balance the interest of making money for himself with making money for you. A bad broker will simply sell you the stuff that pays them the highest commission.

Many brokers are valuable for helping you with financial issues other than selecting investments. If you want a financial advisor to help you in deciding different investment options, get the recommendation of a good accountant. They can point you to clients who have successful investment portfolios. The truth is that you can do this investment thing on your own. The next chapter will help you navigate through it so that you can sail to long-term financial security.

You need to read financial reports, the stocks page, and do lots of studying to invest successfully.

There are investment strategies, such as index investing, that you can walk into with no knowledge about stocks and do just fine. You can put about as much (or little) time into investing as you choose. In fact, you're much better off if you put your money in a safe investment account, and leave it alone instead of checking on it every few hours.

You must have piles of money sitting around in order to justify investing.

Do you have $20 to spare this week? Break that down further: How about $3 a day? You would probably spend that much money on peanuts and a soda at the corner market. If you invest about $3 a day, which is about $1,000 a year, in an investment that averages an 11 percent annual return—the annual stock market return since 1926—it will grow to more than $1 million after forty-six years. For the price of peanuts and a soda, you can watch your money grow and have a financial future that allows you to rest easy and have peace of mind.

The miracle of investment money growth is a result of compounding interest. It works like this: As your money earns investment returns, those returns begin to earn money as well. If you leave your money invested long enough, it keeps mushrooming, while you sit around and do nothing. You don't need to be a financial wizard to realize that this is a better use of your cash than impulse spending or paying late fees at the video rental store. Stocks and mutual funds give you compounding interest (more about these funds in Chapter 11).

FAST FACTS:

The Standard & Poor's (S&P) 500-stock index has increased almost 200 percent since 1970, even after accounting for inflation.

So if you are ready to start investing your hard-earned money so that it can begin to create wealth for you, here are a few things you must do first.

1) *Pay off your credit card debt.* Don't scrape around for money to invest if you have a balance on your credit cards. Pay those off first so you don't have to live

with low credit scores and a rising balance each month. Paying only the minimum payment on your credit card is the equivalent of throwing your money into a sinkhole. High-interest debt carries the same principle as compounded interest. A few dollars of debt can quickly become hundreds of dollars of debt. It makes no sense to invest money while your debts are ballooning.

2) *Establish your cushion fund.* You need to use your money to build up an emergency fund so that you are protected by unexpected financial crises. Only when you have given yourself at least four months' worth of protection should you start investing money. Paying off your high interest debt and establishing your emergency fund are your first priorities before any investing. The exception would be if you are offered a 401(k) plan with a company match. More about this in Chapter 12.

3) *Determine that you will pay yourself first.* If you only invest leftover cash, then you won't do it. You need to decide that investing is a priority, and then pay yourself accordingly. Each month, you pay the electric bill, the phone bill, the babysitter, the nice lady who gives your son piano lessons, and a host of other people and business that provide services for you. Paying yourself should be at the top of that list. Designate a certain amount of money for your investment each month, do it at the first of the

month and automate it so you don't have to labor over the decision.

Investing gives you peace of mind for the future. You can rest easy knowing that your money pile is growing larger each month, and that it will be there waiting for you in the future (near or far) when you need it.

Once you are convinced of the value of investing, you will need to decide how much of your money you want to put away. Remember the beauty of compounding interest? The more you invest the more wealth you create. But don't feel as though you have to choose a big number. Any amount of money that you put into an investment account is going to be better than

DID YOU KNOW?

There are several ways to track the performance of your mutual funds:

- The websites of mutual fund companies
- Financial newspapers and magazines
- Online mutual fund reports
- Year-end mutual fund prospectuses, or official company reports[3]

nothing. If you pay yourself first and automate the investment deposits, you won't even miss it.

Many investment advisors suggest that you invest somewhere between eight and ten percent of your gross annual income. If you can save more, that's great. If you have to opt for less than this, do what you can with the goal of building up the amount over time. If you receive windfall money—a bonus at work, a tax refund, prize money—take a portion (or better, take all of it) and put it in your investment account. Don't forget about that compounding interest. The more money you can get into the investment account, the more it will grow as the returns begin to gain returns.

Another important point about investing: The earlier you begin, the more your money will grow. Maybe you're no longer in your twenties, but if you happen to still be in the early stages of adulthood, you have the potential to grow your money over more years, with more compounding interest. Remember the example about Eve and Bill in the beginning of this chapter. Eve started early, and even though she didn't invest her money as many years as Bill did, she earned more. The reason: The earlier you start, the more years your money has to work that compounding interest magic.

Time is one factor in how much your money will grow. Creating wealth through investing will also depend on the growth rate, which we'll discuss in the next chapter, and how much savings you choose to put into your account each month. You may not have control over the first two factors—time and growth rate—but you have control over

how much you will save each month for your investment
account.

CASE STUDY:

At age 11, **Warren Edward Buffett** bought
his first stock—three shares of Cities Service
Preferred at $38 a share. The price immediately
dropped to $27, but then recovered to $40, and
Buffett sold, making a profit of $5, but missing the
company's subsequent rise to $200 a share. It was
the young investor's first lesson in patience.

Today, after years of being able to spot
undervalued companies and purchase them on the
cheap, the Omaha native has made many people
very wealthy over the course of his five-decade
career. His investing instincts have also made him
quite wealthy. Despite the fact that he lives in a
house he bought for $31,500, he's worth $36
billion, making him the second wealthiest man in
the world. An example of his investment savvy: In
1988, Buffett started buying shares of the Coca-
Cola Company, which was trading at $10.96. He
knew, however, that this product was the world's
strongest brand name and that there was untapped
sales potential overseas. As Coca-Cola's earnings
grew, so did investor interest. In less than five
years, the stock soared to $74.50. Buffet's current
stake in the company is valued at about $13
billion.[4]

PERSONAL REFLECTION:

How has investing given you peace of mind about the future? If you haven't begun to invest, how do you think it would help you worry less about the future?

How many of the myths listed above were included in your own perception about investing? Does knowing they aren't true change your perception?

✓ YOUR TO DO LIST:

Look carefully at your budget. Where could you spend less and save more in order to find money for investing?

Decide on an amount to invest each month (if you have to start small, that's okay), then set up an automated system so that you don't have to make a decision each month about whether to put money in the account. Check with your local bank about automatic investment options.

FOR FURTHER STUDY:

The Wall Street Journal Guide to Understanding Money and Investing
—by Kenneth M. Morris, Virginia B. Morris

The Standard & Poor's Guide to Long-Term Investing: 7 Keys to Building Wealth
—by Joseph Tique.

Straight Talk on Investing: What you Need to Know
—by Jack Brennan

CHAPTER 11

Be Investment Savvy

*Everyone has the brain power
to follow the stock market.
If you made it through fifth grade math,
you can do it.*

—PETER LYNCH

POWER STATEMENT:

Understanding the basics about
the different investment options,
including money market
accounts, CDs, bonds, mutual
funds, and index funds, will
allow you to invest your money
wisely.

Roger's company just gave him a $2,500 Christmas bonus. He is elated, but instead of rushing out to the electronics superstore for an afternoon splurge, he decides to follow his instincts and pay off some debt. Roger has worked to keep his credit card debt in control, but he has accumulated a $1000 balance, so he writes a check to the credit card company and wipes out the high-interest debt. He now has $1,500 left. Once again, Roger has to choose between the electronic superstore and his instincts, which are gently whispering to him that he should invest the money. Roger decides to follow his instincts, and he begins to do some research.

First, Roger must decide what he will eventually do with this money. If he wants to use it for a down payment on a car or for home remodeling, these are short-term goals, and instead of investing his money, he should save it. A short time frame means that Roger wouldn't want to risk that his money could lose its value and not rebound before he needs it. In Chapter 6, we discussed different places to park money that will be used for short-term goals: a passbook savings account, a money market account, or a money market mutual fund.

Roger decided that he wanted to use this money for long-term investment. He had already funded his cushion account for six months worth of salary loss, so he was ready to put his $1,500 in a place where it could grow for a lengthy period of time.

Roger studied all his options:

Certificate of Deposits (CDs) are bank accounts with a fixed time commitment that you choose. You deposit the money in the account and receive a "certificate" that allows you to withdraw the money at a later date—six months, a year, five years. The interest rate is usually higher the longer time frame you choose. If you withdraw early, you will lose a part or all of your interest rate. These accounts can be used for both short-term and long-term investments.

Bonds represent investments in a business—or government or public agency—with a promise of a specific return of your investment in a specific time frame. There are four basic kinds of bonds, all defined by who is selling the debt: bonds sold by the U.S. government and government agencies; bonds sold by corporations; bonds sold by state and local governments; and bonds sold by foreign governments (this last type is usually sold through a mutual fund). These accounts have many of the same attributes as a CD. You deposit the money for a fixed period of time and earn a rate of return—the rates will vary depending on the type of bond you choose. If Roger chooses to invest his money in bonds, he will need to check the rate of return for each kind and take into account the tax consequences when calculating his return. Except for those sold by the federal government, bonds carry the potential risk of default, since there is always a chance that the entity that borrowed the money will not be able to make the interest payment.

Bond index funds are diversified bond funds that invest in both government and corporate bonds. According to financial consultant Jane Bryant Quinn, the younger you are, the less you need bonds, although you always need some for diversification. These funds yield more than a short-term bond fund, but they also rise and fall more in price. If Roger needed to get to his money in five to ten years, a bond index would be a possibility, but he decided that he was willing to leave his money in longer and seek larger earnings. So he began to research the next level of investment.

Stocks represent ownership of a company's assets and profits. A large corporation like IBM has millions of shares of stock outstanding (540 million). Stocks are bought and sold at a "stock market," like the New York Stock Exchange. The price of stock is fixed every second of the day, and therefore the price can fluctuate depending on news from the company, media reports, national economic news— even natural disasters.

Roger thought about investing his $1,500 in an individual stock, but learned that it might not be his best option for a couple of reasons. For one thing, he would have to pay a commission when he bought and sold the stock on the exchange; for another thing, stocks carry risk. If the company he chose had financial or other kinds of problems, he could lose part or all of the money he invested. He discovered that if he chose to put his money in stocks, it would be better to *diversify*. Roger learned about two types of stock investment options, *mutual funds* and *index funds*.

> **FAST FACTS:**
>
> According to the Investment Company Institute, there are about 9,193 mutual funds in existence, roughly 5,196 of which are stock funds.[1]

- A stock *mutual fund* is a pool of stocks owned by a group of investors. These stocks usually consist of three types: growth, value, and blend. *Growth* stocks are shares of companies whose profits and revenues are growing fast. Investors who buy these types of stocks are convinced that these companies' fast growth will cause the price of the stock to go up. *Value* stocks don't involve companies with such a glitzy image. Their share price is believed to be lower than the real value of the company. Investors in value stock use patience to their advantage, and if they feel like the company has long-term prospects, they will hold on to the stock until others in the market start to take notice and buy in. Mutual funds that own stocks that have both growth and value characteristics are called *blend* funds. Most mutual funds are actively managed with a professional whose full-time job is to figure out the best investments for the fund.

- *Index funds* have no money manager who is making buy and sell decisions. An index fund simply tracks an existing market index, which is made up of a number of stocks that represent the market. The Dow Jones Industrial Average and Standard & Poor's 500 Stock Index are two market indexes. Over the years, index funds have outperformed the majority of actively managed mutual funds. These funds charge investors less in fees, which boosts the net return.

After careful research and thought, Roger decided to invest his money in an index market fund. The fees were lower, and he knew that over the long haul, this fund outperformed other types.

Now that Roger had made his decision about where to put his money, he needed to know a few more particulars about investing.

- *Caps.* Each mutual fund usually concentrates on stocks that are one of three sizes: small-cap, mid-cap, or large cap. The caps correlate to the type of companies. Small caps would consist of newer, faster-growing firms; mid-caps are still in the growth stage but have more stability than small-cap; large-caps are the least risky because the firms are large, established multinational companies.

- *Fees.* All funds charge annual fees to cover their operating costs. Typically, a managed mutual fund expense ratio is about 1.8 percent. The expense ratio for an index fund is about .18 percent. The more money you put in, and the longer you leave it in, the more the expense ratio begins to impact your overall earnings.

DID YOU KNOW?

Many studies have shown, that on average, the stock market has an annual return average of 10 percent if you leave money in for a long period of time. Even including stock market crashes, the average remains about 10 percent.[2]

- *Load.* All funds have expense ratios but some also have loads, which is a sales commission used to pay the adviser who sold you the fund. Roger knew that he wanted to get a fund with a no-load in order to maximize earnings, which means that he would have to skip working with a commission-based advisor.

Roger invested his money in an index market fund, and promptly forgot it. He knew that over the years it would grow and he would have the satisfaction of knowing he had made a wise investment.

PERSONAL REFLECTION:

How knowledgeable are you about the different options for investing your money?

Are you a risk-taker, or would you prefer putting your money in something safe that will grow over the long haul?

☑ YOUR TO DO LIST:

Research the different investment options. To learn more about bonds, you can visit www.savingsbonds.gov or www.publicdebt.treas.gov. To learn more about mutual funds, you can visit www.thevanguardgroup.com, www.fidelity.com, or www.troweprice.com.

FOR FURTHER STUDY:

The Little Book That Beats the Market
    —by Andrew Tobias

The Wealthy Barber: The Common Sense Guide to Successful Financial Planning
    —by David Chilton

Kiplinger's Guide to Investing Success: Making Money Today in Stocks, Bonds, Mutual Funds, and Real Estate
    —from the Editors of Kiplinger's Personal Finance

The Neatest Little Guide to Do-It-Yourself Investing
    —by Jason Kelly

Common Sense on Mutual Funds: New Imperatives for the Intelligent Investor
    —by John C. Bogle

CHAPTER 12

Plan for Retirement

*If you depend on your company
to take care of your retirement,
your income will be divided by five.
Take care of it yourself,
and you can multiply your future income by five.*

—JIM ROHN

POWER STATEMENT:

A self-directed retirement plan
involves knowing when and where
to invest so that you will have
money waiting for you when you
decide to retire.

I f you have a picture of how you want to live your retirement years, then you should also have a plan for how you are going to make it happen. The largest contingent ever is marching toward retirement, but people are not saving nearly as much for it as they should. Public Agenda, a public opinion research firm, found that nearly half of Americans (46 percent) have less than $10,000 in retirement savings.[1]

Retirement planning used to be easy. Workers retired at age sixty-five and collected Social Security and an employer pension, then moved to their dream retirement community and lived comfortably. Today, many people want to retire earlier than age sixty-five, and automatic pensions are disappearing and being replaced with self-built and self-directed retirement funds. Social Security is set up to provide about 24 percent of your pre-retirement income—more for lower earners, less for higher earners. Changes in the formula and retirement ages will cause that figure will drop to 20 percent.[2] Don Blandin, president of the American Savings Education Council, says that more households are saying that they are planning for retirement, but most people overestimate how much they will get from Social Security, and underestimate how long they will live.

It's clear that if you want to maintain a comfortable

standard of living after you quit working, you're going to need income beyond Social Security. And since you will be the one deciding how you want to live after retirement, responsible planning for those years is largely up to you.

How Much Will You Need?

Chances are, you won't want to give up your standard of living when you retire. If you enjoy a vacation each year, golf on Saturdays, and driving a decent vehicle, you will still want to enjoy these things after retirement, and so you need to plan to have enough money to maintain your current lifestyle. Financial consultants advise that you should plan for 70 to 80 percent of your gross income. Conservative planners may want to use 100 percent of income as an assumption.

Here is a quick math lesson to bring the amount into reality: Assume that you will need $45,000 on top of a pension benefit of $25,000 for your basic living expenses. Add another $5,000 a year to fund visits to all the grand-kids who are spread out across the country as well as a getaway vacation for you and your spouse. Add it all up, and you will need about $1.2 million to live out your retirement years.[3]

You can plug in your own numbers and calculate an estimate for how much you will need for retirement at Bloomberg.com or Fundadvice.com.

Where Will You Get It?

- 401(k) Retirement Plan

Never turn down free money. If your employer offers a 401(k) or a similar retirement plan and in addition offers a matching contribution, you are being handed free money. About 70 percent of all the people in the U.S, who have the option of opening a 401(k) account at work totally ignore the option. Here's a quick lesson in what a 401(k) is and why you should care about it:

- As an employee, you will contribute your own money to the plan, usually through a payroll deduction. The money in the fund is "tax deferred," which means that you don't pay taxes on it. The interest earned on the money is also tax deferred until you withdraw from the fund.

- The money in the account is invested in a number of mutual funds. As we learned in the previous chapter, mutual funds are safe, they earn a good yield, and they grow relatively quickly.

- If your employer offers a company match, this means your boss will kick in a percentage of your contribution up to a specific amount. If your company match is 50 percent up to $2,000 a year, that means that for every dollar you contribute, your boss will throw in 50 cents, up to the company's maximum. Financial consultant

Suze Orman believes the matching contribution of an employer is so important that contributing to the fund should be at the top of your retirement to-do list. Even if you have credit card debt, or you are trying to save up for a home or a car, you should sign up for your company's 401(k) and invest enough money to get the maximum company match.[4]

- If you leave the company, the money in your 401(k) account still belongs to you, and you can take it with you to your new employer, or roll it over into a personal IRA account (more about that below) where it will continue to earn money, tax deferred.

- Money that is contributed to a 401(k) plan cannot be withdrawn until age fifty-nine without a penalty (you must pay taxes on the money withdrawn, plus you pay a 10 percent fine to the IRS).

If you are still in your young working years and

DID YOU KNOW?

American's increasing longevity means that the next wave of retirees can expect longer retirements than any previous generation. Sixty-five-year-olds who retire in 2015 will face seventeen to twenty-one years of postcareer life on average, with more than one in four living twenty-five more years, according to the Social Security Administration.[6]

convinced that you can't afford the payroll deduction involved in contributing to your plan, look at an example of how a 401(k) would look if you contributed the maximum 15 percent of a $3,000 a month salary (that's $450 a month). If the money grows at 10 percent here's what it would look like—

Year	Account balance
1	$5,655.60
2	$11,906.00
3	$18,813.76
4	$26,448.02
5	$34,885.19
10	$92,401.14
15	$187,228.91
20	$343,573.49
30	$1,026,330.71
40	$2,882,257.27 [5]

- Roth IRA

Unlike the 401(k), the Roth doesn't offer a pre-tax break. Your contribution comes from money that you have already paid taxes on. However, unlike a 401(k), there is no tax penalty when you withdraw your money, as long as you have owned the Roth for a minimum of five years and you are at least fifty-nine at the time you make the withdrawal. With a traditional IRA (another option), the money is also taxed when you withdraw it. Although there are up-front tax breaks with a 401(k) and a traditional IRA, many financial consultants agree that the tax breaks up front aren't as beneficial as the no-tax withdrawal of the Roth, especially if you are in a low tax bracket. Another real-numbers example of the potential growth:

Let's imagine you start investing $4,000 a year in a Roth in 2005, when you are thirty, and you make the same $4,000 investment in 2006 and 2007. Then, assume that all your subsequent annual investments will total a steady $5,000 a year beginning in 2008. If you keep investing in your Roth for twenty-nine years, assuming an 8 percent annual return, you will have $535,480. At the time you are fifty-nine and decide to take your money out, you will pay no taxes, which means you take home all the cash.

There are two catches with the Roth. First, your income can disqualify you from participating. The cutoff is $95,000 for an individual and $150,000 for a married couple filing a joint tax return. Second, there is a maximum contribution level. For the years 2005-2007 you can contribute no more than $4,000, and in 2008, no more than $5,000. In 2009 and beyond, inflation adjustments will be made in $500 increments.

Even with the income and contribution limits, a Roth IRA offers many advantages. Orman suggests that if your employer offers a company match on your 401(k) account, that you contribute to that first, then scrape together enough money to put some cash into a Roth IRA. Together, these two retirement plans will put you on the road to the kind of retirement you can look forward to.

CASE STUDY:

A recent study by Putnam Investments shows that investing prowess isn't what matters. Its how much you sock away. They created Average Joe, a hypothetical twenty-eight-year-old who made the least of his 401(k) between 1990 and 2005. He contributed too little—just 2 percent of his pay, starting at $40,000. By raising his contribution from 2 percent of his salary to 6 percent, Joe would have tripled his 401(k) balance, an almost $8,000 increase.[7]

PERSONAL REFLECTION:

Evaluate your retirement savings plan. If you don't have one, what plans do you have for post-career?

What kind of standard of living do you envision for your retirement? Are you taking that into consideration as you plan?

✓ *YOUR TO DO LIST:*

If you are self-employed, check into SEP IRAs, SIMPLE (Savings Incentive Match Plans for Employees), and Keogh Plans. A financial or tax professional can give you the details.

FOR FURTHER STUDY:

The New Rules of Retirement: Strategies for a Secure Future
—by Robert C. Carlson

How to Build, Protect and Maintain Your 401(k) Plan: Strategies and Tactics
—by Dale Rogers and Craig Rogers

Fairmark Guide to the Roth IRA
—by Kaye A. Thomas

CHAPTER 13

Be Ready for College Tuition

*First, it's the initial outlay for the game system.
But then there's the endless badgering
to supply them with new games to feed their habit.
Sorry, I'd rather put that money
into my son's college fund.*

—MICHELLE SINGLETARY

POWER STATEMENT:

Saving for college tuition doesn't
have to be a budgeting-busting,
anxiety-inducing process if you plan
ahead and know how to invest.

If you have young children, college tuition may be one of the last things on your mind, but financial experts say this is the time to get serious about it. College costs are projected to escalate about 6 percent per year, and some analysts put the price tag of a college education for the parent of today's four-year-olds at $200,000. You have already learned in previous chapters how compounding interest works, so it makes sense that the earlier you budget the money, the easier saving for college is going to be.

Developing a college-savings mindset when your four-year-old is running around the house in Spiderman pajamas may seem impossible, but time has a way of accelerating and before you know it your pajama-clad four-year-old will be heading down the road for the college campus. Here is a money-smart plan for college savings.

Put Yourself First.

This may sound like selfish advice, especially if you are used to putting your children's needs ahead of your own. When it comes to future finances, however, you don't want your children footing the bill for your retirement. If you have to make a choice right now between putting money back for retirement and saving for college, choose a retirement fund. Your children can get a loan for college, but no one will loan you the money for retirement. Once you have a retirement fund going, you can begin a college savings plan.

Save Something

If you have begun a nice retirement nest egg, you can turn your attention to saving for your children's education. Don't be fooled by the argument that savers qualify for less college aid. Financial experts agree that part of your aid comes in the form of loans, and people without any savings have to borrow more. That's no good. If you have an income level that would allow you to save but you chose not to (you bought home theater systems and fancy cars instead), you won't find college-aid officers very sympathetic. Those who save something, anything, are always better off.

The 529 Plan

529 savings plans are college savings trusts set up under Section 529 of the IRS—hence the name. Within certain guidelines, each state can set up a trust managed by an investment company.[1] You can invest in any state's plan, but each plan is a little different and some states' fees are higher than others, so you'll have to do a little research. If the plan is expensive and you don't get state tax breaks, look for a state with low fees and solid investment choices. Three states with low-cost plans are Ohio's College Advantage 529 Savings Plan, Utah's Educational Savings

Plan Trust, and Virginia's Education Savings Trust.

You can purchase a plan directly from the state (called "direct-solid plans") or buy through a stockbroker or planner ("advisor-sold plans"). Both types are listed on the state websites. Buying from the state is free and easy—just fill in a form, pick your investments, and mail a check. The plans offer several options for investments, including an all-stock fund, a fixed-income fund, a mixed stock and bond fund, and several age-related choices.

Financial experts agree that you should start saving as early as possible. In a few states, your money might have to remain in the plan for two to four years before it can be withdrawn. In most states, however, you can start a 529 plan when your child is seventeen. You can contribute up to a total of $200,000 or $300,000 per child, depending on the state. If your child gets a scholarship and doesn't need all the money you have invested in the plan, you can take out the money equal to the scholarship amount and pay taxes on the earnings, but no penalty. You can also keep the account and name a new beneficiary.

More Savings Plans

Most financial experts agree that the following college savings plans don't compare to the 529, but they are worth mentioning:

- *Coverdell Education Savings Account (ESA).*
  This account works like a 529, but you can
  only contribute $2,000 a year for each
  child up to his or her eighteenth birthday.
  There are no state tax breaks on the money
  invested; however, you can use the money
  for the expenses of private school—
  kindergarten through twelfth grade—or
  equipment needed for public school, such
  as a laptop.

- *U.S. Savings Bonds.* If you are twenty-four
  years old or over and have bought Series
  EE bonds issued since January 1990, you
  can use the proceeds, tax-free, toward the
  cost of higher education for yourself,
  spouse, or dependent. Your income must
  fall within a certain limit during the year you
  want to redeem the bonds, however. For
  more info, go to Savingsbonds.gov.

- *An Individual Retirement Account.* You
  won't have to worry paying the penalty on
  an early withdrawal if you use the money in
  your IRA account to pay for higher
  education.

Tax Relief

The IRS offers tax credits and deductions to help offset
some college costs. They are typically only available for
families with gross income under $130,000, $65,000 for
single parents.

- *Hope Scholarship Credit* is a credit up to $1,500 a year per student for qualified education expenses (not including living expenses) during the first two years of school.

- *Lifetime Learning Credit* gives a credit of 20 percent of the first $10,000 of qualified expenses (tuition and fees) for a maximum credit of $2,000 per family. This credit and the Hope Scholarship Credit have a $4,000 cap per year per family.

- *Student loan interest* is deductible (up to $25,000) against income, if income qualifications are met.

Grants and Loans

A variety of aid plans are offered or supported by the federal government, most in the form of grants or loans. Grants are based on need, and usually aren't paid back. Loans may or may not be based on need, and must be paid back. Pell and Supplemental Educational Opportunity Grants are the two major federal grant programs, and recipients can receive from a few hundred dollars to $3,000 (Pell) or $4,000 (SEOG) per year. Both depend on family need.

FAST FACTS:

On average, tuition tends to increase about 8% per year. An 8% college inflation rate means that the cost of college doubles every nine years.[2]

Loan programs consist of three types:

- *Perkins loans* can benefit families with high need and can finance expenses up to $20,000 (undergraduate) or $40,000 (graduate) with a maximum interest rate of 5 percent. Payments are deferred until graduation.

- *Stafford loans* provide increasing amounts as a student progresses through college. Loan limits are up to $10,500 a year for under-graduates and $18,500 a year for graduate students. Interest rates won't exceed 8.5 percent, although the loans are made through private institutions which could mean large origination fees.

> ## DID YOU KNOW?
>
> A monthly deposit of $50 made over fifteen years, assuming a 6 percent investment return, provides $14,540, enough to a pay at least a year of college costs (depending on inflation).[3]

- *Parent Loans to Undergraduate Students (PLUS)* are made to parents of students and have variable interest rates that don't exceed 9 percent. They can originate at private institutions or through the U.S. Department of Education. The balance of the loan is limited only by education cost, and may be paid off in part through public service.

If you choose the best savings vehicle, you can prepare for college tuition while your child is preparing for a college education.

PERSONAL REFLECTION:

If you have children, do you have a plan to pay for their college education?

Are you expecting to depend on grants and loans, or are you willing to chip in some investment savings?

☑ YOUR TO DO LIST:

Get the detailed and comparative information on all the 529s on the Web: Savingforcollege.com, or call the College Savings Plan Network (Collegesavings.org; 877-277-6496).

FOR FURTHER STUDY:

The Best Way to Save for College: A Complete Guide to 529 Plans
—by Joseph F. Hurley.

C H A P T E R 14

Know How to Buy a House

*But to every thing there is a time
and a season,
and that's as true for home buying
as it is for everything else.*
—JUNE FLETCHER

POWER STATEMENT:

Buying a house can be an
emotional and exciting
experience, but it is important to
understand types of mortgages,
home equity and how to
navigate the buying process.

B uying a house involves more than just choosing a sturdy structure that you can afford. For some people, the home is an opportunity to express creativity and personality. For others, it's where they take refuge from the world. Because a home is much more than bricks and mortar, purchasing one can become an emotional experience where smart financial decisions get lost in the desire for picket fences, dormer windows, and a garden spot in the backyard.

Enjoying your home for years to come, however, means that you will want to use money smarts when you decide to purchase. If you have decided that it is time to buy a house, here is what you need to do:

Get your financial house in order.

Banks tend to be careful about loaning out large dollar amounts to people who might not be able to pay back the loan. Before a bank hands over the money to you, they require you to do these four things:

- Have cash on hand for a down payment, usually 5 or 10 percent of the home's purchase price. In addition, you will need to have cash for closing costs, which are the fees you pay to close the loan.

- Have a job that pays a steady annual income and prove that your monthly mortgage payments will not eat up most of your income. The bank has two tests for this: *the allowable monthly housing cost test,* and *the allowable total monthly debt payment test.*

- Have a good FICO score.

- Have an acceptable balance sheet and net worth.

In addition to what the bank will require, you should have some standards of your own that you meet before you launch out and purchase your dream home:

- Pay down all your high-interest debt, or make sure that it is in rapidly declining mode.

- Be enrolled in and contribute the maximum to your company's matching 401(k) plan, or be actively funding a Roth IRA account (or both).

- Have a cushion fund set up that will provide four to six months of income.

Be realistic about how much house you can afford.

Just because the bank will loan you $300,000 for a house doesn't mean that you can afford a $300,000 house. Somewhere down the line you may decide to send your kids to private school or buy a pontoon boat or travel to Paris every year, and you may lament funneling all your extra cash into a mortgage payment. Friends and family may advise you to buy more house than you can afford, but life is unpredictable. There is no guarantee that in two years you will be able to afford a house that is above your means any more than you can afford it right now.

The general rule of thumb is that a mortgage payment should be no more than 28 percent of your gross income, although according to financial consultant Peter Sander, this rule has flexed a bit in recent years. He gives this example: If your earnings are $75,000 a year, then 28 percent of that figure would be $21,000 a year, or $1,750 a month. At a 6 percent interest rate for thirty years, that payment works backward into a loan amount of $291,885. If you choose to put 20 percent down, that gives a maximum affordable value of $364,856.[1]

You should, however, take into consideration that the monthly mortgage payment is not your only expense as a homeowner. In deciding how much house you can afford, you should also include property tax, homeowner's insurance, private mortgage insurance, and maintenance. Can you afford to lump all of these additional expenditures in with your mortgage payment without shortchanging your retirement fund or other important goals?

Choose your mortgage carefully.

You will have to choose the type and term of your mortgage. The *term* refers to how long you will take to pay off the loan. Most terms are fifteen or thirty years, with a few at ten and twenty years. A traditional thirty-year mortgage carries low monthly payments, but most of your payment goes toward interest. If you are on a tight budget or are a first-time home buyer, this is the term you will probably want to choose. A fifteen-year mortgage has higher monthly payments, but you get a lower interest rate and can retire the loan in a shorter amount of time. Less of your payment goes toward interest, which is a good way to put more money in your own pocket.

There are two main types of mortgages: *fixed* and *adjustable*. With a fixed mortgage, interest rates and payments remain unchanged for the life of the mortgage. Adjustable mortgages have variable interest rates and, therefore, variable payments depending on the prevailing interest rates. The adjustable mortgage does have a "cap", but you will have no control over how much and when your payments will climb. The initial low interest rate of the ARM may be alluring, but you could get caught with a mortgage payment that you cannot pay if you aren't prepared for the hike in your monthly payment.

Think carefully about your down payment.

If you borrow more than 80 percent of the value of the home, most lenders will require PMI—private mortgage insurance. This protects the lender in case you are unable to repay the loan. PMI adds to the cost of your home, so avoid tacking on this additional payment if possible. What that means is that you will need to put down 20 percent if you want to bypass PMI. Not everyone can afford to do so, but if you have the cash on hand, it will save you money in the long run.

DID YOU KNOW?

In 2005, a resident of La Jolla, California could sell his home and buy fourteen identical ones in Killeen, Texas, and still have more than $36,000 left in his pocket. A Coldwell Banker Home Price Comparison Index found that a 2,200-square-foot, four-bedroom, two-and-a-half bath, two-car garage home in Killeen cost just $131,328, compared to a similar home in La Jolla for $1,875,000—more than fourteen times as much. According to Money magazine, the findings underscore the biggest truth in real estate: The three most important factors in home buying are location, location, location.[3]

Protect your home equity.

Your home equity is the difference between your

home's market value and the size of your mortgage. The more equity you have in your home, the wealthier you are.

According to financial expert Jane Bryant Quinn, there three ways for equity to grow. 1) During real estate booms, eager buyers bid the prices up. 2) During normal times, home prices stay flat or rise modestly while you lower your mortgage by paying off a little debt each month. 3) You make improvements to the property.

There are also four ways to lose your equity. 1) Home prices fall. 2) You borrow more money against your home by refinancing into a larger

FAST FACTS:

Home buyers pay eight times the closing costs they paid forty years ago.

mortgage, or you take a home equity loan. 3) You fail to maintain your property and it falls into disrepair. 4) You run into financial trouble, can't repay the loan, and lose the property. You should do everything possible to grow and protect your home's equity.[2]

Decide whether to pay additional points.

A point is 1 percentage point of your loan amount. If you want to reduce your mortgage interest rate and your monthly payment, you can pay points. When you do this, you are essentially paying your interest early. A lender may require you to pay two to three points at closing, and because of tax reasons, it's better for you to pay them at closing instead of rolling them into the mortgage. If you want to pay additional points, consider that it may not be worth it if you are going to be in the house for only a few years.

Be ready for closing costs.

After you have found your dream house and negotiated a contract, you will come to the table to close the deal. Be prepared for the costs that are involved. National averages

CASE STUDY:

Ed and Blanche had built up equity in their house thanks to a real estate boom in their area. Unfortunately, they were strapped with over $15,000 in credit card debt, so they decided to take a home equity line of credit (HELOC) to pare that down. Although they knew they should be protecting their equity at all costs, they figured they would be able to pay off the HELOC and wipe out their credit card debt. The HELOC's adjustable rate caught them unaware, and the payments increased after a few months. They found themselves unable to keep up with the payments, and they were forced to sell their home. They realized that putting their home at risk in order to pay off unsecured credit card debt was an unnecessary trade-off that had set them years behind financially.

for closing costs are about $3,650. Depending on where you live and the price of your home, this figure could double. When you are deciding how much house you can afford, you should take into consideration the additional cash it will take just to get the deal done.

Money Smart Home Buyer's Checklist:

- Get your financial house in order
- Decide how much home you can afford
- Decide on the term and type of mortgage
- Put as much down as you can
- Protect your equity

PERSONAL REFLECTION:

If you own a home, how are you protecting your equity? Are you maintaining your home and continuing to pay down your mortgage? Or are you skimping on home maintenance and taking out home equity loans?

If you are thinking about buying a home, are you realistic about how much house you can afford?

✓ *YOUR TO DO LIST:*

If you are preparing to buy a home, check interest rates and fees at these websites: Elaon.com, Indymac.com, and Mortgage.com. Look at the regular ARMs and fixed rate loans, and ignore the interest-only ARMs and Option ARMs.

If you have a year or more to prepare for the purchase of your first home, get your financial house in order by checking your FICO score (annualcreditreport.com), and then commit to improving your score if necessary. You can do this by paying your bills on time, reducing your high interest debt (pay down those credit card balances!), and keeping your credit card bills low in the months before you apply for a mortgage.

FOR FURTHER STUDY:

Mortgages 101: Quick Answers to Over 250 Critical Questions About Your Home Loan
    —by David Reed

The New Complete Book of Home Buying
    —by Michael Sumichrast, Ronald Shafer, Martin Sumichrast

Home Closing Checklist
    —by Robert Irwin

Get on with Life

*A wise man should have
money in his head,
but not in his heart.*
—JONATHAN SWIFT

POWER STATEMENT:

Once you have put the money laws
into place, you can live life without
worrying and obsessing over
finances.

In her book *The Nine Steps to Financial Freedom* Suze Orman tells the story of a trip she took to Mexico and her encounter with a parrot seller. The parrots were lined up on a perch, none of them trying to escape. When Orman asked the merchant why the parrots weren't flying away, he told her that he had trained them to think their perches meant safety and security. When they think this, he said, they naturally wrap their claws tightly around the perch and don't want to release it. They keep themselves confined, just as if they had forgotten how to fly.

Orman says that a light bulb went off in her head, and she realized that we are like those birds, taught to clutch our money as tightly as we can, as if it is the perch of our safety and security. When she asked the merchant how he

DID YOU KNOW?

Studies have shows that investors who tune out the majority of financial news fare better than those who subject themselves to an endless stream of information. According to Gary Belsky and Thomas Gilovich, authors of *Why Smart People Make Big Money Mistakes*, the less frequently you check on your investments, the less likely you'll be to react emotionally to the ups and downs of the securities markets. For most investors, a yearly review of your portfolio is frequent enough.[2]

would go about teaching the birds to unlearn this behavior, he replied that it would be easy. He would just show them how to release their grip, and then they would be able to fly wherever and whenever they pleased.[1]

Not only do we grip our money tightly, but at the same time, our money grips us as well. We worry about losing it, not making enough of it, not having enough to spend. We budget every penny with feverish anxiety, wring our hands over the stock market, and refuse to enjoy life because of the money we might have to spend. Instead of being in control of our money, our money is in control of us.

You can't ignore the importance of money. Zig Ziglar once said, "Money isn't the most important thing in life, but it's reasonably close to oxygen on the 'gotta have it' scale." This is true. We all must have money to survive, and the more you have, the easier it is to survive. But we cheat ourselves out of enjoying the other things life has to offer when we make money our singular focus. Many people live unnecessarily frugal lives, says Andrea Orr, writing in the *Stanford Business Magazine*. They are fearful of not having enough, but saving excessively at the cost of leading a comfortable and rewarding life can be a form of overly emotional investing. Baba Shiv, an associate professor of marketing at Stanford says that frugal people take joy in seeing money accumulate. This behavior can become compulsive and detrimental.

Then there are people who dedicate inordinate amounts of time to spending their money. Shopping, ordering, planning the next purchase, and juggling the balances on multiple credit cards becomes a time-consuming endeavor.

The money-smart laws in this book are designed to put you in control of your money. If you follow them, you have the satisfaction of knowing you have done your best to manage, protect, and grow your money. Then you can turn your attention to the other things in life that really matter.

PERSONAL REFLECTION:

What is your biggest money fear? In what ways has your money been controlling you?

YOUR TO DO LIST:

Choose the money laws that you need to put into place right now in order to gain control over your money. Commit to letting go of your money worries as you put the laws into place.

FOR FURTHER STUDY:

The Nine Steps to Financial Freedom: Practical and Spiritual Steps So You Can Stop Worrying
—by Suze Orman

The Soul of Money: Transforming Your Relationship with Money and Life
—by Lynne Twist

APPENDIX A
Net Worth Worksheets

ASSETS
Cash and Liquid Assets

Checking Account	$
Savings Account	$
Certificates of Deposit	$
Money Market Account	$

Total =

Investments	
Treasury Bills	$
Stocks	$
Bonds	$
Mutual Funds	$
Real Estate	$
IRA (Traditional/Roth)	$
401(k), 403(b), Pensions	$

Total =

Personal

Automobiles/Vehicles	$
Home Furnishings/Appliances	$
Antiques/Collectibles	$
Value of Life Insurance	$
Value of Personal Business	$
Jewelry	$
Other	$

Total =

Total Assets =

LIABILITIES

Debt

Credit Card Debt	$
Child Support	$
Alimony	$

Total =

Loans

Vehicle loans/lease	$
Loans against investments or insurance	$
Student loans	$
Personal Loans from family/friends	$
Other	$

Total =

Mortgages

Primary Home	$
Secondary Home	$
Land	$

Total =

Total Liabilities =

CASH FLOW

Skip any line that doesn't apply. Don't forget to include car costs such as insurance, gas, maintenance, repairs and parking fees, in addition to your loan payment.

Car	$
Vacations	$
Utilities	$
Telephone/Cable/Internet	$
School	$
Savings	$
Personal Care (dry cleaning, haircuts, etc)	$
Medical (not covered by insurance	$
Insurance (life, health, home, liability)	$
Housing (mortgage or rent)	$
Home Improvement or furnishings	$
Groceries	$
Gifts	$
Entertainment	$
Credit Card payment	$
Clothing	$
Charity	$
Child Care	$
Other	$
Total	$

APPENDIX B

Sample Budgets

Budget #1

Category	Monthly Budget	Amount Spent	Difference
INCOME			
Wages/Bonuses			
EXPENSES			
Home			
Mortgage/Rent			
Homeowners/ Renters Insurance			
Property Taxes			
Repairs/Maintenance			
Improvements			
Utilities			
Electricity			
Water/Sewer			
Telephone			
Natural Gas			
Internet			
Cable/Satellite			
Food			
Groceries			
Dining Out			
Children			
Child Support			
Daycare			
School Tuition/Fees			
Health/MedicaL			
Insurance			
Fitness Clubs			
Medical Copays			
Transportation			
Car payment			
Gas			
Repairs/Maintenance			
Insurance			
Parking fees/tolls			

Debt			
Credit Cards			
Student Loans			
Other Loans			
Entertainment			
Movies			
Recreation/Hobbies			
Vacations			
Gifts			
Pets			
Food			
Vet/Grooming			
Clothing			
Charitable Contributions			
Investments/Savings			
Miscellaneous			
Total Investments and Expenses			
Surplus or Shortage			

Budget #2

Category	Monthly Budget	Amount Spent	Difference
Income			
Expenses			
Groceries			
Utilities			
Mortgage/Rent			
School Expense			
Child Expenses			
Medical Expenses			
Pets			
Car Payment			
Gas			
Entertainment			
Charitable Contributions			
Miscellaneous			
Total Expenses			
Surplus or Shortage			

NOTES

Chapter 1

[1] Michelle Singletary, "Use Your Net Worth as a Starting Point." *Washington Post*, January 12, 2006.

[2] Singletary, "Starting Point."

[3] Moyer, Liz. "The Myth of the Cashless Society." *Forbes*. Web article: http://www.forbes.com/2006/02/11/cashless-society-cash_cx_em_money06_0214cashless.html.

[4] Christopher Conkey, "Typical U.S. Family's Net Worth Edged Up Only 1.5 % in '01-'04," *The Wall Street Journal*, 24 February 2006, sec. A, p. 4.

Chapter 2

[1] Lawrence, Judy, *The Budget Kit* (Chicago: Dearborn Trade Publishing, 2003), 23.

[2] Cybele Weisser, "Take Charge." *Money*, October 2004, 82.

Chapter 3

[1] *Personalbudgeting.com*: http://personalbudgeting.com/tips/tips.html.

[2] *CNNMoney.com*: http://money.cnn.com/pf/101/lessons/2/

Chapter 4

[1] Web article: "What Causes Customers to Buy on Impulse?": http://www.uie.com/publications/whitepapers/ImpulseBuying.pdf

[2] Stanley, Thomas and Danko, William, *The Millionaire Next Door* (New York: Pocket Books, 1996), 7.

[3] Jeanne Sahadi, "The Ultimate Money Challenge." *CNNMoney.com*: http://money.cnn.com/2004/10/26/commentary/everyday/sahadi/index.htm

4 Marshall Brain, "Understanding and Controlling Your Finances: Frugality." Web article: http://bygpub.com/finance/

5 Jennifer Mulrean, "7 Radical Ways to Save Money", *MSN Money* web article: http://moneycentral.msn.com/content/Savinganddebt/Savemoney/P36019.asp

Chapter 5

1 *CNNMoney.com*: http://money.cnn.com/pf/101/lessons/9/

2 Taura Lynn Colbert, "Managing Your Money: Lesson 3—Looking for New Directions." Web article: http://www.suite101.com/lesson.cfm/18823/2694/2

3 Suze Orman, *The Money Book for the Young, Fabulous and Broke* (New York: Riverhead Books, 2005), 119-120.

4 Orman, *Young, Fabulous and Broke*, 95-96

5 David and Tom Gardner, *The Motley Fool Personal Finance Workbook* (New York: Simon and Schuster, 2003), 27-28.

6 Jane Bryant Quinn, *Smart and Simple Financial Strategies for Busy People* (New York: Simon and Schuster, 2006), 46-47.

7 Orman, *Young, Fabulous and Broke*, 86-87.

Chapter 6

1 Martin Crutsinger, "Americans Saving Very Little," *Seattle Post Intelligencer*, 31 January 2006.

2 Crutsinger, "Americans Saving Very Little."

3 Quinn, *Smart and Simple*, 23.

4 Poll from the GE Center for Financial Learning, "Spotlight on Finances." Web article: http://rentaldecorating.com/1102spotlightfinances.htm.

5 Orman, *Young, Fabulous and Broke*, 150.

Chapter 7

1 Peter Sander, *The 250 Personal Finance Questions Everyone Should Ask* (Massachusetts: Adams Media, 2005), 45.

2 Orman, *Young, Fabulous and Broke*, 261.

3 Web article: http://www.fpanet.org/public/tools/lifeevents/purchases-bigticket.html.

4 Orman, *Young, Fabulous and Broke*, 255.

Chapter 8

1 Quinn, *Smart and Simple*, 83.

2 Gardner, *The Motley Fool Personal Finance Workbook* p. 49

3 Marshall Brain, "Understanding and Controlling Your Finances." Web article: http://bygpub.com/finance/finance10.htm.

4 Jeanne Sahadi, "Retiree Health Costs up 5.3 percent." *CNNMoney.com*: http://money.cnn.com/2006/03/06/retirement/health_costs/index.htm.

5 "Nine Ways to Save on Your Auto Insurance Policy." Web article: http://info.insure.com/auto/autosave.html.

Chapter 9

1 Pat Regnier and Amanda Gengler. "Men, Women and Money" Money April 2006, 90.

2 Teri Brown, "The Dollars and Sense of Marriage," *IParenting.com*: http://iparenting.com/resources/articles/marriagedollars.htm.

3 Regnier and Gengler, "Men, Women and Money," 96.

4 "The Key to Meeting Your Money Goals." *CBSNews.com*: www.cbsnews.com/stories/2006/01/10/earlyshow/living/money/main194310.shtml

5 Web article: http://www.jumpstart.org

6 Web article: www.themint.org/about/adultsprove

7 Web article:
   http://www.themint.org/about/whatkidsdontknow.php

Chapter 10

1 Lois Center-Shabazz, *Let's Get Financial Savvy* (Chesapeake, VA: CenNet Systems Publishing, 2003), 33.

2 Gardner, *Motley Fool*, 69.

3 Motoko Rich and David Leonhardt, "In the Long Run, Sleep at Home and Invest in the Stock Market." *New York Times*, 19 August 2005:
   http://www.nytimes.com/2005/08/19/realestate/19real.html.

4 Larry Kanter, "The Oracle of Omaha." *Salon.com*, 31 August 1999: http://www.salon.com/people/bc/1999/08/31/buffett/

Chapter 11

1 "Ask the Fool," *Tulsa World*, 3 April 2006, sec. A, p. 11.

2 Marshall Brain, "Investment Options." Web article:
   http://bygpub.com/finance/finance8.htm.

Chapter 12

1 Web article: http://hffo.cuna.org/guides/retire1.html.

2 Sander, 250 *Personal Finance Questions*, 74.

3 Michael Sivy, "How You'll Pay For It," *Money*, November 2005, 105.

4 Orman, *Young, Fabulous and Broke*, 184.

5 Marshall Brain, "Understanding and Controlling Your Finances." Web article: http://bygpub.com/finance/finance6.htm.

6 Matthew Heimer and Kristen Bellstrom, "Retire Happy," *Money*, April 2006, 65.

7 Walter Updegrave, "How Even Average Joe Can Retire Rich." *Money*, January 2006, 50.

Chapter 13

[1] Sander, *250 Personal Finance Questions*, 65.

[2] Web article: http://finaid.org/savings/tuition-inflation.phtml.

[3] Sander, *250 Personal Finance Questions*, 70.

Chapter 14

[1] Sander, *250 Personal Finance Questions*, 55.

[2] Quinn, *Smart and Simple*, 101.

[3] Gandel, Stephen, "Closing Cost Scams," *Money*, March 2006: http://money.cnn.com/2006/02/13/real_estate/closingcosts_mo ney_0603/index.htm.

Chapter 15

[1] Suze Orman, *The 9 Steps to Financial Freedom*: Practical and Spiritual Steps So You Can Stop Worrying (New York: Crown Publishers, 1997), 262-263.

[2] Gary Belsky and Thomas Gilovich, *Why Smart People Make Big Money Mistakes and How to Correct Them* (New York: Simon and Schuster, 1999), 206.